Japanese Quilt Blocks to Mix & Match

Japanese Quilt Blocks to Mix & Match

Over 125 patchwork, appliqué and sashiko designs

Susan Briscoe

A&CB

Contents

A QUARTO BOOK

First published in the UK in 2007 by
A & C Black Publishers
38 Soho Square
London W1D 3HB
www.acblack.com

ISBN-10: 0-7136-8246-9
ISBN-13: 978-0-7136-8246-5

Conceived, designed and produced by
Quarto Publishing plc
The Old Brewery
6 Blundell Street
London N7 9BH

QUA: JQB

Editor: Michelle Pickering
Art editor: Natasha Montgomery
Designer: Helen Crawford-White
Photographers: Karl Adamson, Paul Forrester
Illustrator: Kuo Kang Chen
Assistant art director: Penny Cobb

Art director: Moira Clinch
Publisher: Paul Carslake

Colour separation by Modern Age Repro House Ltd, Hong Kong
Printed by SNP Leefung Holding Ltd, China

9 8 7 6 5 4 3 2 1

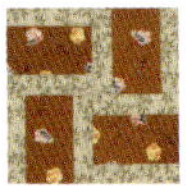

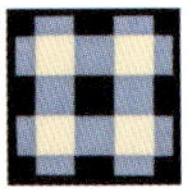

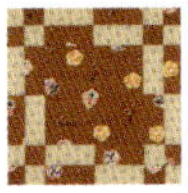

Sashiko Blocks

Kamon Blocks

Takarazukushi Blocks

Introduction

Patchwork and quilting have become very popular in Japan over the last 30 years. Initially inspired by Western traditions, many Japanese quilters combine Japanese designs with Western patchwork and quilting to create quilts with a unique look. This book is a resource for creating that unique look in your own projects.

Japanese block designs

This book features more than 125 block designs, all of which have been drafted from traditional Japanese pattern sources. There are complete instructions and a clear photograph for each block, as well as at-a-glance symbols indicating the techniques used and ability level required – there are blocks for beginners as well as more advanced quilters. All the techniques are clearly explained with step-by-step photographs, from cutting the first pieces to finishing your quilt.

Colours and fabrics

Traditional Japanese fabrics, including kimono, provide the inspiration for both the designs and colours of the blocks, from the exotic motifs to the striking hues. Fabrics include Japanese and oriental-style patchwork fabrics, as well as plains, shot cottons and geometric patterns. The Japanese colour schemes include taupe browns, indigo and white, antique, and kimono colours, from restful low contrasts to the dazzling vibrancy of unexpected combinations.

LEFT & BELOW

This bright 1970s random patchwork juban (under-kimono) inspired block 82.

LEFT & BELOW

Contemporary kimono often use antique colour schemes, like this hōmongi (visiting kimono) and block 64.

LEFT & BELOW

The colourful ikat pattern of this 1930s meisen silk kimono is re-created in patchwork in block 8.

Mixing and matching blocks

All of the blocks can be mixed and matched and combined in sampler quilts, and many will tessellate for all-over patterns. Suggestions for combining the blocks are given throughout the block directory, and you will find a selection of sampler quilts, cushions and bags in the gallery. These will give you ideas for your own quilt layouts, so you can use the book to design and create unique quilts with a Japanese style. Have fun!

LEFT
Mix and match the blocks in the directory in any combination to create beautiful quilts, wallhangings and throws.

Block categories

Patchwork These include geometric patterns (top left) as well as pictorial designs (top centre).

Sashiko Meaning 'little stab' or 'little pierce', sashiko (top right) was traditionally stitched on work clothes and household textiles to make them warmer, stronger and more hardwearing. Everyday sashiko was plain, but sashiko for special occasions featured elaborate designs. Old sashiko uses mostly blue and white combinations, but nowadays sashiko is stitched with other colours.

Kamon Kamon are traditional family crests, and can be stitched as sashiko (bottom left) or worked as appliqué (bottom centre).

Takarazukushi These collection of treasures and good fortune symbols are worked as appliqué (bottom right).

How to Use This Book

At the beginning of the book you will find an illustrated contents list showing all the blocks. Look through the list, find some blocks you like and use them as the starting point for your quilt.

Block size

The finished size of all the blocks in this book is 9 in. (22.9 cm) wide when they are sewn together to make a quilt top. The actual size of each block is 9½ in. (24 cm) wide with seam allowances. A ¼ in. (6 mm) seam allowance is used throughout. Most blocks are also 9½ in. (24 cm) long, so they are square. However, patchwork blocks with hexagons, diamonds and equilateral triangles are 10¾ in. (27.3 cm) long, including the seam allowances, to accommodate the 60-degree angle and enable the blocks to tessellate. These blocks may be cut down to 9½ in. (24 cm) square, or you could use sashings and border strips to equalize the sizes of the blocks.

Mix and match

The book starts with an inspirational gallery of quilts, wallhangings, cushion covers and bags made from the blocks in the directory. These provide ideas for using the blocks in different arrangements, as well as fabric and colour variations. You will find additional mix-and-match ideas for combining the blocks throughout the directory.

Quilt layouts

Each gallery item and mix-and-match idea is accompanied by a list of the blocks used to make it.

Techniques

This section has detailed information on equipment and techniques, including step-by-step photographs showing how to construct different kinds of blocks, in patchwork, appliqué and sashiko. At the end of the section, there is information on how to finish your quilt, from assembling the quilt top to basic quilting and binding.

Non-quilt ideas

You can use the blocks to make items other than quilts, so the gallery also includes some wallhangings, cushion covers and bags to inspire you.

Step-by-steps

All of the techniques required to make the blocks are explained step-by-step.

Block directory

The block directory contains all the cutting and construction information for each block, with a photograph, fabric selection, cutting list, construction method and at-a-glance symbols. Imperial and metric measurements are given. Follow either imperial or metric measurements throughout – don't switch between the two. Remember that the cutting list specifications includes ¼ in. (6 mm) seam allowances.

Understanding the symbols

Every block design has at-a-glance symbols indicating the skill level, technique and tessellation possibilities.

Skill level

Easy

Intermediate

Advanced

Technique

Patchwork

Appliqué

Sashiko

Tessellation

Blocks can be combined to make an all-over pattern

Patchwork diagrams

The patchwork construction diagrams show the order in which you should piece the patches together.

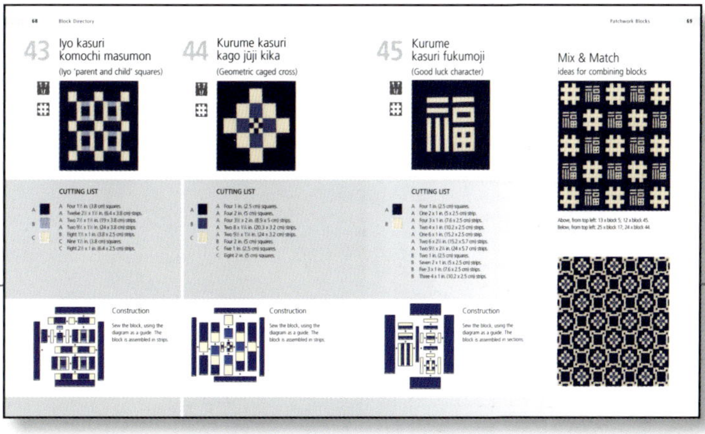

Mix & match ideas

Throughout the directory you will find ideas for arranging the blocks in different ways. Sometimes blocks may be assembled as a mirror image or turned through 90 degrees for a different effect. These illustrations show quilts made without sashings or borders, and include possibilities for tessellation.

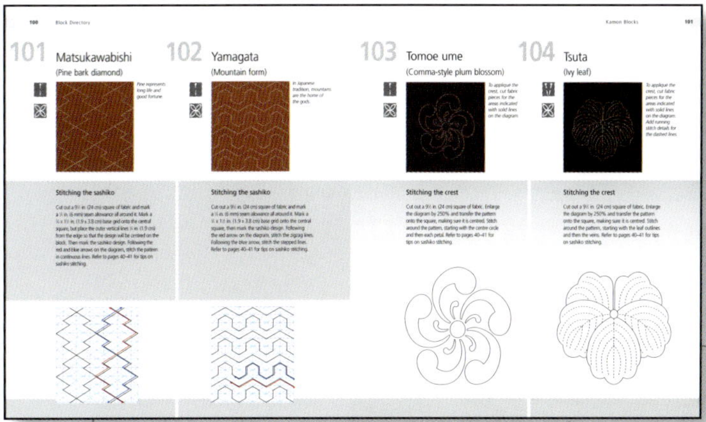

Kamon and takarazukushi diagrams

All kamon and takarazukushi diagrams are shown at reduced size, so you will need to enlarge them on a photocopier by the specified percentage before you begin. You will need the diagram on a separate sheet to trace the pattern onto the background fabric, either to stitch as sashiko or for positioning appliqué pieces accurately. After tracing, cut out individual templates for the appliqué pieces.

Sashiko diagrams

Sashiko diagrams show the base grid in blue, as listed in the instructions. Stitching lines are shown as solid black lines. If the base grid is stitched as part of the design, it appears as a solid black line, too. Coloured arrows indicate the stitching sequence and direction.

Gallery

The finished pieces in this section were all made using the blocks in this book. You can copy them if you wish, or use them as inspiration for your own ideas. Experiment and enjoy!

LEFT

Patchwork blocks and appliqué kamon (family crest) designs in bright colours are combined in this sampler quilt. Sashing strips, cut from shaded fabric, give an optical illusion of weaving. The blocks used, from top left, are: 118, 124, 115, 125, 79, 120, 63, 73, 66, 119, 67, 71, 65, 75, 62, 114, 74, 82, 72, 116, 121, 124, 117, 122 and 78.

OPPOSITE

Repeating block 38 in different fabrics, including stripes, produces a quilt with wonderful variety, which is heightened by staggering the columns of blocks. The subtle blues and browns echo antique Japanese country textiles.

LEFT

Takarazukushi (collection of treasures) designs assembled with bright blue sashing are the focal point of this quilt centre. Their rich colours reflect Taishō era (1912–1926) designs. The quilt uses blocks 126–132 in a random order.

OPPOSITE

All these traditional patterns are featured in Hakone yosegi parquetry designs, so they suit the taupe colour scheme. Each block is bordered individually and the quilt is assembled in columns. The longer isometric blocks at the top and bottom of alternate columns produce a staggered horizontal line. The blocks used, from top left, are: 1, 60, 28, 59, 26, 52, 35, 29, 13, 53, 36, 12, 55, 34, 49, 50, 54, 56, 27, 39, 58, 3, 61, 57 and 64.

RIGHT

Yukari Domon used block 39 with hand-appliquéd flowers to make this beautiful bag. She cut vintage checked fabric to create the shaded effect in the block. The bag was pieced and quilted by hand.

LEFT

Geometric sashiko blocks on blue, black and brown cotton show a rich variety of designs. Simple sashing cut from striped fabric looks three-dimensional and emphasizes the white stitches. The blocks used, from top left, are: 92, 85, 96, 91, 98, 101, 99, 84, 94, 83, 93, 86, 90, 87, 102, 88, 97, 95, 100 and 89.

OPPOSITE, BELOW LEFT

Julie-Elizabeth Haslam tessellated and extended block 62 for this cushion front in English paper piecing. The gold, pink and black colour scheme is from vintage kimono.

RIGHT

Sashiko expert Chie Ikeda used vintage stripes and indigo cotton for this adaptation of blocks 17 and 39 as a cushion cover. The corners of block 17 are made from squares, to use up scraps, and the completed block is used as the centre piece for an enlarged quarter of block 39. The plain indigo patches are decorated with Shōnai-style sashiko.

BELOW RIGHT

Another pillow panel in English paper piecing by Julie-Elizabeth Haslam, combining modern oriental patchwork prints and extending block 63.

LEFT

Autumn colors inspired Diane Abram's kamon (family crest) banner, machine appliquéd with metallic threads and oriental patchwork prints. The golden edges are reminiscent of kinkoma embroidery and the blocks are quilted in Diane's prize-winning style. The blocks used, from top down, are: 106, 123 and 108; the crest from block 111 adorns the tip.

BELOW

Aiko Sakuraba incorporated vintage kimono fabric in this sophisticated bag. The flap is made with block 49 and the bag was pieced and quilted by hand.

OPPOSITE

This snowy scene is created with geometric and pictorial patchwork blocks. The kimono block at the bottom is repeated in blue and brown prints to balance the design. The blocks used, from top left, are: 7, 76, 77, 6 and two versions of 68.

RIGHT

This quilt uses the strong, sophisticated colours that were the height of fashion in the Taishō era (1912–1926). Sashing on two sides of each block and multicoloured borders keep it lively. The blocks used, from top left, are: 33, 38, 32, 4, 48, 69, 51, 25, 31, 24, 47, two versions of 37, 30, 68, 22, 69, 2, 38 and 33.

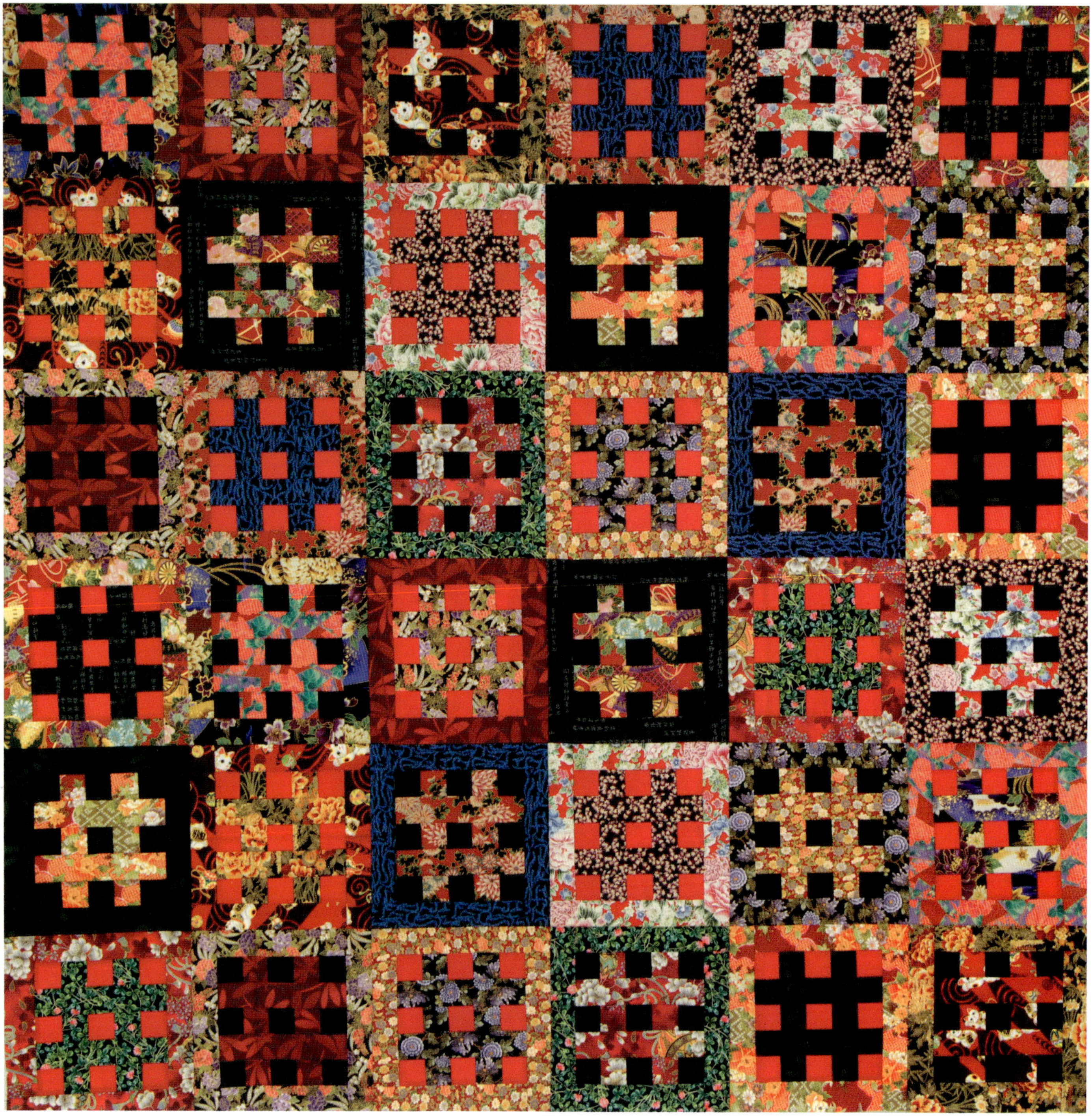

OPPOSITE

Block 5 repeated in different fabrics, alternating black and red print backgrounds, with wider borders on each block, makes a rich and colourful quilt.

RIGHT

This sampler quilt, alternating patchwork kasuri designs with sashiko kamon (family crests), uses the checkerboard arrangement seen on old kasuri futon covers. The quilt is assembled without sashing. The blocks used, from top left, are: 5, 103, 45, 111, 10, 114, 19, 105, 11, 112, 44, 104, 42, 106, 9, 109, 23, 107, 20, 108, 17, 120, 14, 110, 15, 118, 43, 113, 40, 115, 16, 123, 18, 124 and 5.

Materials, Tools and Techniques

In this chapter you will find guidance on choosing fabrics and colours for creating a Japanese or oriental-style quilt, plus ideas on getting the most from different textile designs and how to calculate fabric requirements. You will also find a comprehensive summary of the techniques needed to piece and join the blocks in the directory, and an overview of the equipment required.

Fabric

The use of fabrics and colours is one of the most striking features of Japanese quilts. To help you choose fabrics, try basing your quilt scheme on an old kimono or Japanese print.

Japanese traditions

The modern wave of Japanese quilt making has developed its own styles and uses Western terms. However, patchwork, appliqué and quilting were already part of Japan's rich textile tradition. For more than a thousand years, valuable pieces of cloth have been recombined to make special items, while humble homemade fabrics were patched together for everyday reuse. Items included kesa (monk's robes, from the 10th century onwards), komebukuro (rice bags for gift giving), hyaku toku ('hundred virtues' children's kimono from Kanazawa), dōnuki (under-kimono from two-layer sets) and hanui (patchwork kimono worn for the Nishimonai festival in Akita Prefecture). Fabrics from worn-out clothing were salvaged and remade as patchwork donza and noragi (work jackets), often with added sashiko. Vintage fabrics are the inspiration for many modern patchwork fabrics by Japanese and Western designers, so we no longer need antique scraps but can get the same look at our local quilt shop.

ABOVE & RIGHT

Modern hyaku toku-style kimono made from antique kasuri, stripes and checks by Izuho Horiuchi and early 20th-century silk bags, all hand-pieced.

LEFT & BELOW

The style of patchwork used in this 1920s silk and rayon dōnuki under-kimono is reproduced in block 73.

ABOVE & RIGHT

The kasane kikkō pattern from this 1970s patchwork-effect stencilled haori (kimono jacket) was used as the design for block 65.

Types of fabric

The easiest fabric to use for patchwork and appliqué is 100 percent cotton, which can be pressed to give a crisp seam. Most vintage Japanese fabrics are reproduced as cotton prints, often with dobby or sateen weaves for textural interest. Prints vary from tiny designs to large-scale patterns, and Japanese quilts often combine both. Speciality Japanese quilt stores in the West also sell fabrics in traditional narrow kimono width – 14½ in. (37 cm) – either in silk, cotton, or wool, as well as fabrics salvaged from damaged kimono. Think twice before cutting up an old kimono for patchwork yourself – you may have an interesting antique, and vintage kimono are a finite source of patchwork material.

Woven patterns Traditional cotton fabrics with woven patterns suitable for patchwork include shima (stripes), kōshi (checks), kasuri (ikat) and tsumugi (a slubbed weave). Tsumugi is also woven in silk, can be crisp or soft, and is pleasant to sew if you have experience with silk. Thin meisen silk is no longer made, but old meisen is also beautiful for patchwork, in stripes, kasuri or blurry dyed patterns, often in vivid colours. Indian shot cottons are similar to meisen. Cotton reproductions of all these fabrics are made for patchwork. Shijira ori, a crinkly cotton similar to seersucker, is popular with Japanese quilters. American cotton stripes and checks blend in well for the Japanese country look, although the dark blue is often more ultramarine than indigo.

Shima stripe cotton

Kurume kasuri cotton

Kōshi check cotton

Kasuri cotton

Dyed patterns Dyed patterns vary between large- and small-scale designs. Freehand yūzen rice-paste resist dyeing continues to be used for high-class formal kimono, often on rinzu silk damask, sometimes with silk or gold embroidery. Komon (small patterns) are traditionally stencilled. Edo komon patterns are tiny stencilled designs in two colours, similar to tone-on-tone patchwork fabric. Soft recycled kimono silks, like chirimen (crepe), can be backed with a lightweight iron-on interfacing for patchwork. Woven silk obi fabric, like Nishijin ori from Kyoto, is too thick to use for patchwork, although Japanese quilts sometimes use this fabric for borders. Many gold-print quilting fabrics look similar. Patchwork cotton prints of all these fabrics are available.

Edo komon silk

Yūzen silk

Stencil-dyed cottons Stencil-dyed cottons, like yukata for summer casual kimono, are good for patchwork. Modern women's designs are usually very large prints. Men's yukata favour smaller geometric patterns. Katazome, large-scale stencilled fabric, used to be made for household textiles like futon covers and is now reproduced for quilting. It is usually indigo and white. Patchwork prints of shibori (tie dye) and kasuri (ikat) provide affordable copies of expensive fabrics. Modern sashiko fabric is woven to imitate old handwoven cotton.

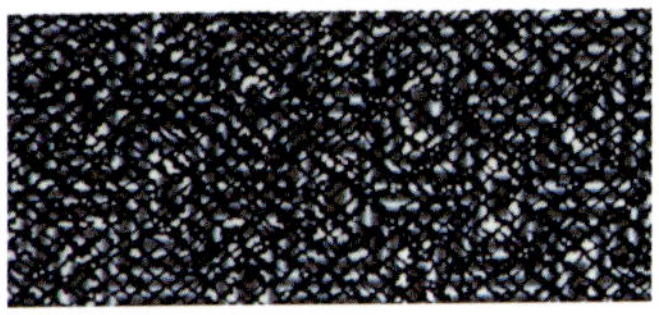

Men's yukata cotton

Ladies' yukata cotton

Modern and antique katazome cottons

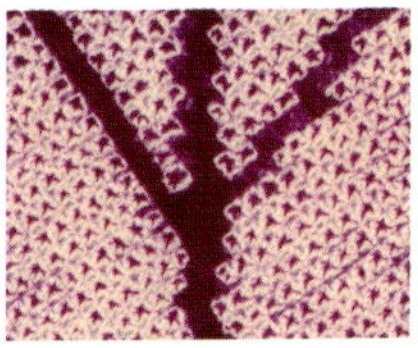

Shibori silk

Colour Schemes

Popular colour schemes include taupe (sepia), indigo and white, Taishō antique, and bright kimono colours. Some quilters recycle old kimono fabrics, but these designs are now reproduced in patchwork cottons, so it is possible to have the best of both worlds – easy-to-piece cotton with the beauty of traditional designs.

Hakone yosegi parquetry dish

Taupe

Various browns, greys and beige are very popular for Japanese quilts and are easy to combine successfully. American country-style fabrics blend in well. Blocks in this colour scheme are all patterns from Hakone yosegi parquetry.

Indigo and white

Different shades of plain indigo and creamy white, including reproductions of katazome stencil-dyed patterns, are very popular. Old kasuri fabric is becoming too scarce to be readily used in quilts. Blocks in this colour scheme are all based on vintage kasuri ikat weaving designs.

Rice bag made from ikat fabrics

Leaf green 1920s irotomesode kimono with Taishō antique colours in the skirt panels

Calculating fabric quantities

For a rough idea of how much fabric you need, note down how many blocks you want to make, then the sizes and number of pieces for each fabric. Multiply these together. For example, if you need four 2 in. (5 cm) squares for each block and there are 20 blocks, you will need 80 squares. To cut these in four rows of 20 squares across 42-in. (105-cm) wide fabric would require 8 in. (20.3 cm) of fabric. If the fabric is 'fussy cut', selecting a particular motif or stripe direction, you will need more fabric. If you do not have enough of one fabric, substitute a similar tone.

Taishō antique

This colour scheme includes tertiary colours with plain rust. Taishō-era (1912–1926) women's kimono have large, bold patterns with sophisticated colour schemes, including vivid leaf greens, plum, russet and dead-leaf yellow. Blocks in this colour scheme have traditional geometric patterns and include miniature kimono.

Kimono colours

The fresh colours of girls' and boys' ceremonial kimono provide a wide choice of patchwork fabrics with pretty floral and geometric patterns. Accent them with red and gold metallics. Blocks in this colour scheme include kamon (family crests), geometric patterns and miniature kimono. Miyamairi kimono are used like a christening shawl.

Meisen geometrics

These include bright colours, shot cottons and plaid. Meisen weaves often have different colours for warp and weft. Many of the patchwork quilt blocks in this book interpret geometric meisen silk designs.

1960s girl's miyamairi kimono

1970s boy's miyamairi kimono

1920s meisen silk kimono

Design tips

- Small-scale fabric prints will disguise patchwork seams, while larger patterns emphasize the piecing. Changing just one fabric can give a block a very different look.
- Cut out individual fabric motifs, such as large flowers or leaves, and appliqué them onto your blocks.
- Cutting appliqué designs from one piece of fabric, with the pattern passing from one part of the appliqué to another, gives a traditional look. Outlines of flowers, leaves and other objects dyed on kimono are often filled in with other patterns.
- Seasonal floral motifs are used slightly in advance of their season in Japan, apparently because flowers on fabric cannot compete with the real thing. However, stylized flowers and leaves can be used at any time. Multiple-season flowers in one pattern can also be used all year long.
- Traditionally, sashiko is not stitched through wadding, but may be backed with a piece of old fabric – try loosely woven muslin.

Equipment

Tools and materials for making Western quilts can also be used to make Japanese quilts, and there are some extra items that will give your quilting experience an authentic oriental flavour.

Scissors

Use fabric scissors for cutting fabric, embroidery scissors for cutting threads, and paper scissors for cutting templates. Nigiri basami (finger scissors) are sharp thread snips that can be used for trimming threads.

Pins and safety pins

Select fine pins, such as dressmaking or silk pins, for piecing patchwork. Flat-headed (or flower-headed) pins are useful for machine sewing because the flat head stops them from twisting in the fabric. Use safety pins to hold the layers of a quilt together as an alternative to tacking stitches.

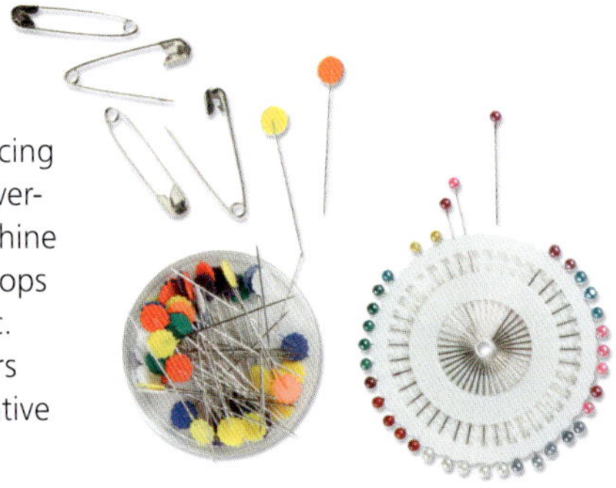

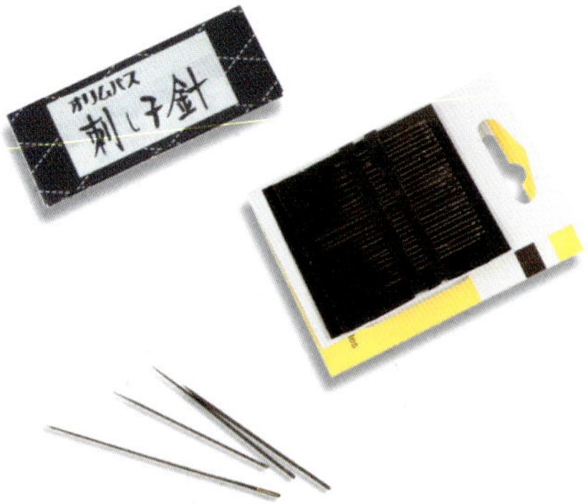

Needles for hand sewing

Use 'sharps' (long, thin needles) for hand piecing, appliqué and tacking. Use sashiko needles, which are long and rigid, for sashiko stitching. Use 'betweens' (short, sturdy needles) or smaller sharps for hand quilting.

Threads

Medium-thickness (50s) cotton sewing thread is best for piecing; choose a neutral colour that blends with the fabrics. Select thicker (30s or 40s) cotton thread for machine or hand quilting. Special quilting threads include variegated and metallic threads (the latter require a metallica machine needle). Hand-quilting threads are treated to resist knotting. Other threads can be treated with beeswax or silicone wax; simply pull the thread over the edge of the wax block several times. Sashiko threads are loosely spun, traditionally white, but now available in colours.

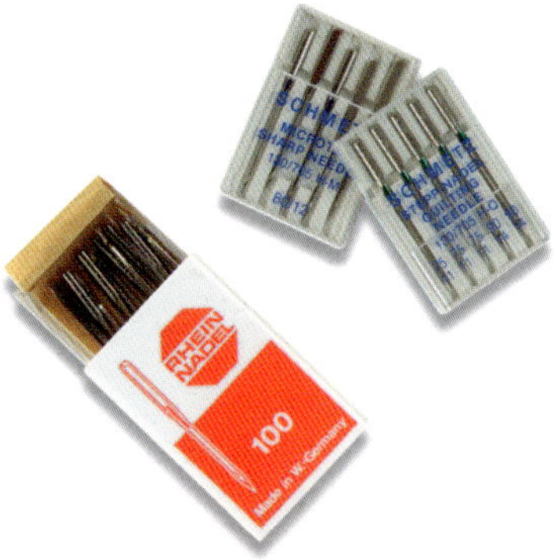

Needles for machine sewing

Universal needles in size 70 or 80 (European) – 10 or 12 (US) – are good for machine piecing. Quilting needles are sharper and best for machine quilting. Try Microtex for finer fabrics and silks.

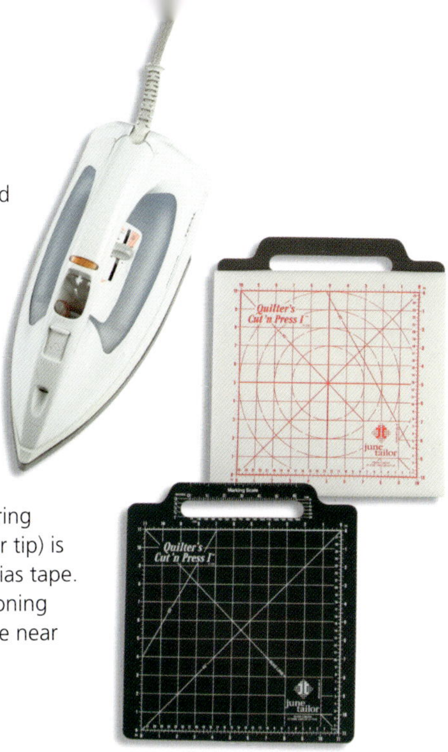

Iron and board

An ordinary iron and board is fine for pressing blocks. Use the appropriate temperature setting and avoid steaming blocks during piecing because this can distort the seams. Steam-pressing finished blocks or quilt tops is fine. A small travel iron or a mini appliqué iron (like a soldering iron with a small triangular tip) is best for applying fusible bias tape. A pressing mat or small ironing board is convenient for use near the sewing machine.

Ruler

Rulers are made in many different shapes and sizes. A rectangular ruler about 14 in. (35 cm) long and 4½ in. (11.5 cm) wide with 60-degree and 45-degree markings is fine. A 9½ in. (24 cm) square ruler is good for squaring up finished blocks. Look at the line markings and choose colours you will be able to see against the fabric. Use the same make of ruler whenever possible, because measurements can vary slightly between manufacturers and between the ruler and mat – always double check.

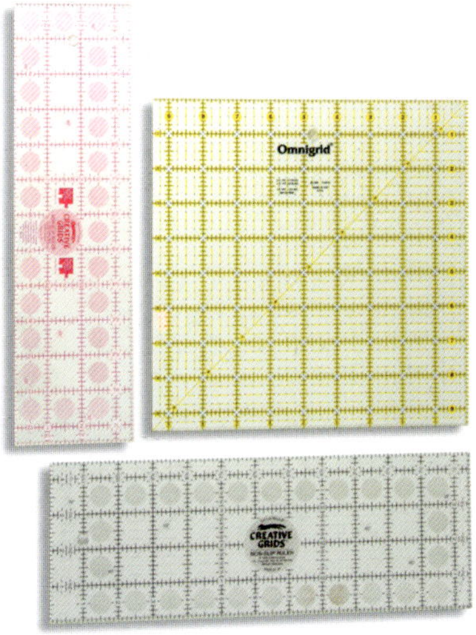

Rotary cutter

A cutter with a 28 mm or 45 mm blade will be most useful (blades are sold in metric sizes only). Try out several cutters to find one that feels comfortable. The blades are razor sharp, so always replace the blade guard after cutting and never leave the cutter where children or pets can reach it. The cutter must be used with a self-healing cutting mat.

Self-healing cutting mat

A large mat is best, such as 18 x 24 in. (45 x 60 cm); smaller mats make cutting difficult. Choose a mat with a printed measurement grid, either imperial or metric, depending on the system you prefer.

Sewing machine

Useful features for patchwork and quilting include a good straight stitch and a needle-down option. A ¼ in. (6 mm) patchwork foot is essential for accurate machine piecing. For machine quilting, a walking foot (for straight lines) and a darning foot (also called an embroidery foot or quilting foot, for free-motion quilting) will be necessary. A large space under the machine arm will allow for easier machine quilting.

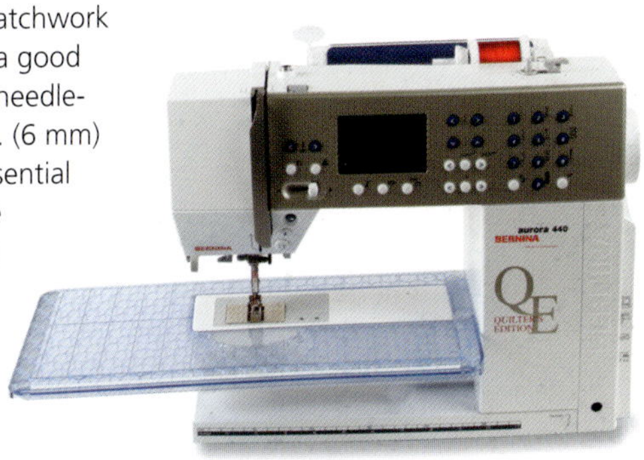

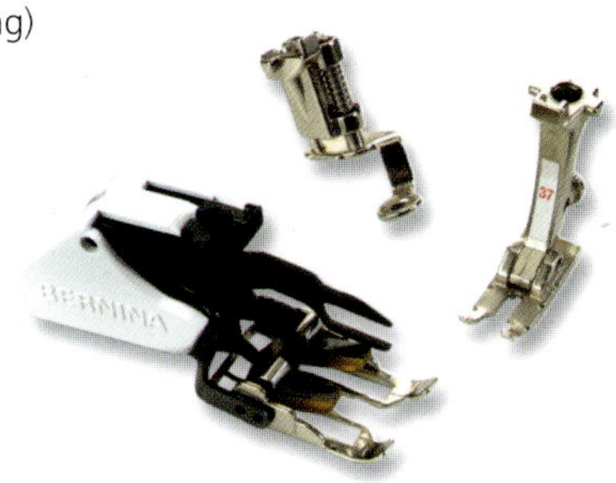

Cutting

Rotary cutting the pieces of fabric for your blocks will be more accurate than using scissors. It is also quicker because you can cut through more than one fabric layer at a time. Make cutting easier by pressing the fabric first, especially any folds. All of the measurements in the block directory include a 1/4 in. (6 mm) seam allowance.

Strips

With the ruler firmly on top of the fabric, square off uneven ends and cut off the tightly woven selvages. Fold the fabric if required, and line up the relevant measurement on the ruler with the straight edge of the fabric. Place the rotary cutter against the ruler's edge and cut. Cut with the straight grain of the fabric wherever possible; with printed stripes and checks, cut with the pattern.

Squares and rectangles

Cut strips into squares and rectangles by aligning the ruler in the same way as before and cutting across the strip of fabric.

Triangles from squares and rectangles

1 Cut squares in half along one diagonal to make a half-square triangle, lining up the 45-degree angle on the ruler with the edge of the square.

2 Cut again for quarter-square triangles.

3 Cut rectangles in half in the same way as squares, but check the instructions carefully because sometimes the diagonal line should slope to the right and sometimes to the left.

Equilateral triangles, diamonds and mitres

Cut 60-degree triangles and diamonds from a strip of fabric using the angle lines on the ruler. You can use the same techniques to mitre edges for parallelograms, trapezoids and quadrangles, using the 45-degree line on the ruler and adjusting the distance and orientation between the first and second cuts as required.

1 To cut an equilateral triangle, align the 60-degree line on the ruler with the bottom edge of the strip and cut. Pivot the ruler so that the other 60-degree line is on the bottom edge of the strip and cut again.

2 To cut a diamond, cut the first edge at 60 degrees as before. Keeping the 60-degree line on the ruler aligned, slide the ruler along the strip until the required measurement aligns with the first cut edge (for diamonds, this should equal the width of the strip) and cut again.

Hexagons and isometric shapes

The easiest way to cut hexagons is to use a template made from isometric graph paper, which is marked with 60-degree triangles. This can also be used to cut diamonds and equilateral triangles.

1 Cut out a hexagon shape, with each side equal to the required measurement. You can use isometric paper to make templates for 60-degree diamonds and triangles as well.

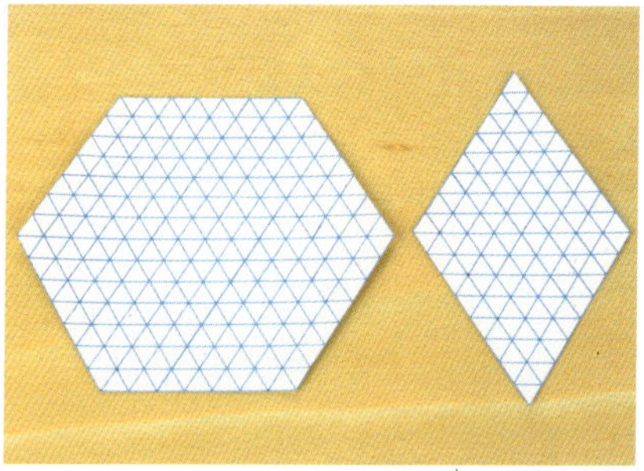

2 Temporarily stick the template to the underside of the ruler using transparent tape, lining up the edge of the template with the 60-degree line on the ruler. Cut out the required shapes from a strip of fabric, lining up the template and ruler for each cut.

Cutting safety

The rotary cutter has a very sharp blade and it is easy to cut yourself or others accidentally, so:

- Hold the cutter firmly at a 45-degree angle in the hand you write with; hold the ruler in place with your other hand. Keep the blade upright against the edge of the ruler.
- With the fabric under the ruler, cut the required piece with the blade against the side of the ruler, on the right if you are right-handed and on the left if you are left-handed.
- Stand up to cut if you can and place the mat on a firm surface, such as a kitchen counter or sturdy table.
- Use a sharp blade that is free from nicks and other damage; a dull blade requires more pressure to cut, with the risk that the blade will slip.
- Always cut away from yourself.
- Always replace the safety guard on the cutter after every cut.
- Wear something on your feet in case you drop the cutter.
- Keep cutting equipment away from children and pets.

Piecing

Machine-sewn patchwork is relatively quick to do. Set the stitch length to 12–14 stitches per inch (2.5 cm) – that is, about 2–1.7 mm long. If you prefer hand piecing, draw a guideline in pencil, then sew the seam along the guideline using very small running stitches with an occasional backstitch; start and finish with several backstitches. Use a ¼ in. (6 mm) seam allowance throughout, whichever method you use. Contrasting coloured threads have been used here for clarity.

Laying out the pieces

Always lay out the pieces of the block in the correct order before you begin sewing; this will help you to avoid joining the pieces together in the wrong order. Many patterns, such as block 5 shown here, require pieces to be sewn together in rows first.

Machine sewing

Place the first two pieces right sides together, making sure the edges to be sewn align. Align the fabric edges with the edge of the ¼ in. (6 mm) machine foot and sew the seam; it may help if you sit slightly to the right of the machine needle so you can see this easily. Use a fabric scrap as a 'leader', so that the first patchwork stitches do not get chewed up. Pin longer seams together at right angles to the stitching line and remove the pins as you sew.

Chain piecing

Chain piecing speeds up sewing patchwork. When you have sewn the first two pieces together, do not cut the thread. Place the next two pieces together and sew them a stitch or two after the first two pieces. Continue like this to make a 'chain', then snip the threads between the pieces in the chain afterwards.

Quick piecing

To make patterns like block 3 quickly by machine, sew long strips of fabric together, then press and cut into segments of the required length. For example, if individual rectangles are 1½ x 3½ in. (3.8 x 8.9 cm), cut long 1½-in. (3.8-cm) wide strips of fabric, sew them together, then cut 3½-in. (8.9-cm) long segments. This method is also used to create the hexagons for block 64. The pieces must be machine sewn because the first seams are cut through and hand sewing would come undone.

Pressing patchwork

Press each stage of your patchwork as you go along, with the seam allowance to one side; this will help to stop the wadding from 'bearding' – coming through the seams. Press towards the darker fabric out of preference, because pressing dark towards light can cause a shadow effect on paler fabrics. Pressing in alternate directions makes the seams interlock neatly, as shown. For designs pieced from the centre outwards, such as blocks 24 and 25, press the seams towards the outside of the block if you prefer. Press with a dry iron or just a little steam, using an up-and-down action so that the patchwork is not stretched and distorted – you are pressing, not ironing. Good pressing can really make a difference to your patchwork, so get it right before you continue piecing.

Sewing tip

Replace the standard zigzag throat plate on your machine with a straight stitch plate for patchwork and quilting. The needle cannot be accidentally dragged sideways with this plate, giving a better straight stitch. Consult your machine dealer for more information, and remember to replace the zigzag plate afterwards.

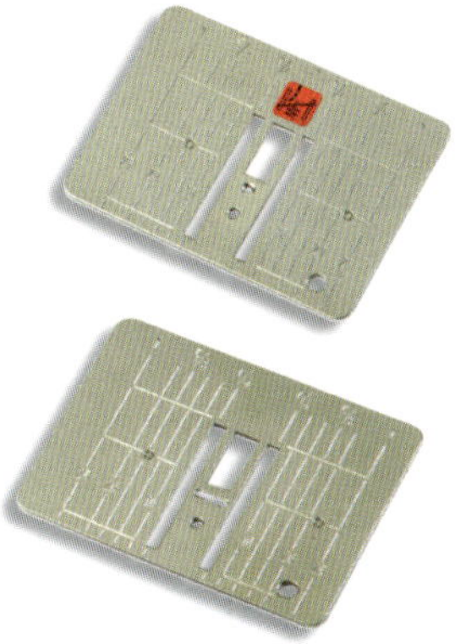

Inset seams

Inset seams are required when two patchwork pieces form a mitre and another piece has to be sewn into that angle and cannot be sewn in place in a straight line.

1 Mark the seam allowance at each corner point with a dot.

2 Sew the first two pieces together between the dots. Start sewing by stitching back towards the dot, then sew between the dots, then reverse stitch again to finish.

3 Insert the next piece in the same way, marking and sewing between the dots on both seams. Patterns built up using inset seams include blocks 65 (shown here), 66 and 67. Press all the seams either clockwise or anticlockwise.

English paper piecing

Sewing hexagons, diamonds, triangles and other mitred shapes together is easier with English paper piecing.

1 Cut paper templates to the exact finished size of each piece (that is, excluding seam allowances) and tack the fabric patches around them, sewing through the paper.

2 With right sides together, oversew or whipstitch the pieces together, starting and finishing the sewing with a knot about ¼ in. (6 mm) from the corner of the patch.

3 Insert the next piece in the same way. Press the patchwork when complete and carefully remove the papers and tacking stitches.

Sewing mitres

Sew the 45-degree mitres required for designs like block 32 in a similar way to fast corners (page 37).

1 Align the corners of the two pieces right sides together and mark a 45-degree diagonal sewing line. Pin together, checking that the pieces are positioned correctly, then sew along the drawn line.

2 Open out the joined pieces, press the seam and trim away the excess fabric. Continue joining pieces with 45-degree mitred joins as necessary.

Part-sewn seams

The arrangement of strips around a central square copies a feature seen in Japanese architecture and flooring. Designs such as block 38, shown here, require the first seam to be only partly sewn.

1 Place the first rectangle and the central square right sides together and line up the first seam. Machine sew, but only sew half of the seam (red thread).

2 Press the seam allowance towards the rectangle, then add the next rectangle. Sew the whole seam this time, then press the seam allowance towards the rectangle again. Continue in this way until the final rectangle has been added, then complete the first part-sewn seam.

3 Press the seams of the block in the usual way.

Piecing a circle

Kamon crests are often traditionally used within a light circle against a dark background. With a little practice, piecing is much quicker than appliquéing a circle as a background for kamon.

1 Make one 8-in. (20.3-cm) diameter and one 7-in. (17.8-cm) diameter circle template from card stock or template plastic. Draw balance marks around the edge like compass points – north, northeast, east and so on – on each template. Centre the 7 in. (17.8 cm) template on the backing fabric, draw around it, transfer the balance marks and cut out the circle. Cut out an 8 in. (20.3 cm) circle from the second fabric, again transferring the balance marks.

2 With the background fabric on top and right sides together, align the balance marks. Pin these points first, then add more pins around the curve. Machine sew the two pieces together, easing around the curve. Open out and press the seam towards the background (outer) fabric.

Triangle squares

This accurate method of making a triangle square avoids the necessity of sewing two bias-cut edges together, because the cut is made after the diagonal lines are sewn. Use it to make designs like blocks 28 and 29. For greater accuracy, add an extra ⅜ in. (1 cm) seam allowance to the desired finished size of the triangle square – for example, cut 4⅞ in. (12.4 cm) squares to make a 4½ in. (11.4 cm) triangle square. The measurements in the block directory include this extra allowance.

1 Draw a diagonal line on the lighter square and place the squares right sides together. Treat this line as the fabric edge, lining it up with the edge of the ¼ in. (6 mm) machine foot. Machine sew along each side of the drawn line, then cut along the line.

2 Open out both triangle squares and press the seams towards the darker fabric. Trim the ends of the seams flush with the edges of the squares.

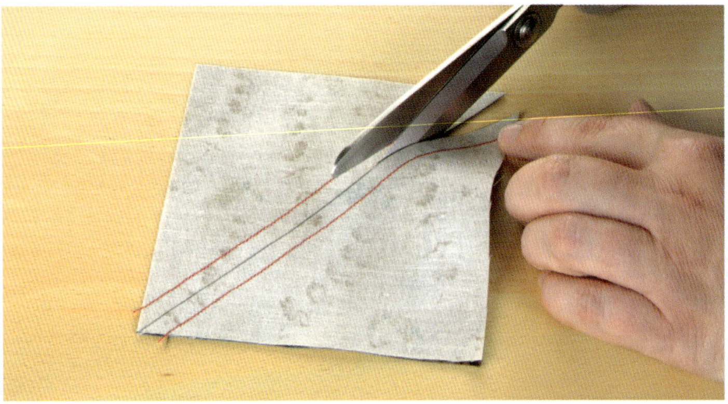

Fast corners

This is a quick and easy way of adding triangles to the corners of a larger patchwork piece, such as block 27. Cut out a square of the required size and draw a diagonal line across it on the wrong side. Place the square right sides together on the required corner and sew along the drawn line. Fold over the triangle you have made and press. Trim away the excess fabric underneath and repeat at each corner.

Special piecing techniques

Blocks 74 and 75 require some additional piecing techniques.

1 To add the corner triangles for the Mount Fuji section of the blocks, lay two triangles on the background fabric, lining up the corners. Draw along the diagonal edges of each triangle with a ruler. Remove the triangles to draw a second diagonal line parallel to the first, ½ in. (1.3 cm) under where the triangles were positioned. With right sides together, align the diagonal edges of the triangles with the second drawn lines, so that the triangles will align with the corners of the rectangle when opened out, and sew. Fold over the sewn triangles and press. Use scissors to trim away the excess fabric underneath each triangle.

2 For the Torii gate, appliqué the bias tape in place on the sky section of the block to form the 1-in. (2.5-cm) long vertical and 7-in. (17.8-cm) long horizontal bars of the gate. Sew the sky, mountain and foreground sections together. Cut the block on either side of the mountain, sloping inwards from 2 in. (5 cm) in at the bottom edge to 2½ in. (6.4 cm) at the top. Insert the two strips for the sides of the gate.

3 Fold the strip that forms the top of the gate in half widthways. Cut the ends at an angle, then cut a gentle curve towards the centre along one long edge. Appliqué to the top strip of sky at the short ends. Appliqué bias tape along the raw curved edge (page 39). Lay out the pieces, sew the sides of the gate into the bottom section of the block, then add the top section.

Appliqué

Appliqué involves laying and stitching one piece of fabric over another to create a decorative design. It is excellent for kamon crests and for adding details to patchwork blocks. Appliqué can be sewn by hand or machine, or fused in place prior to machine sewing.

Needle-turn appliqué

Also known as template-free appliqué, this method gives a firm, strong edge to the appliquéd shape and is popular with Japanese quilters. You will need to add an ⅛ in. (3 mm) turning allowance all around each piece.

1 Tack the shape to the background with small stitches ¼ in. (6 mm) from the cut edge. The tacking stitches will prevent too much fabric from being turned under.

2 Use an appliqué needle or a long sharp to turn under the raw edge a little at a time as you sew, using the point of the needle to stroke the fabric edge into place. Come up through the very edge of the appliqué shape and down through the backing fabric. Start and finish sewing on a long edge, sewing the shape to the background with small hemming stitches. As most of the appliqué shape will have a bias edge, it is not necessary to clip the fabric on a curve; just ease it under. Only clip into deep V shapes, and even then only by a few threads of fabric. Press the turned edge between your fingers as you go along.

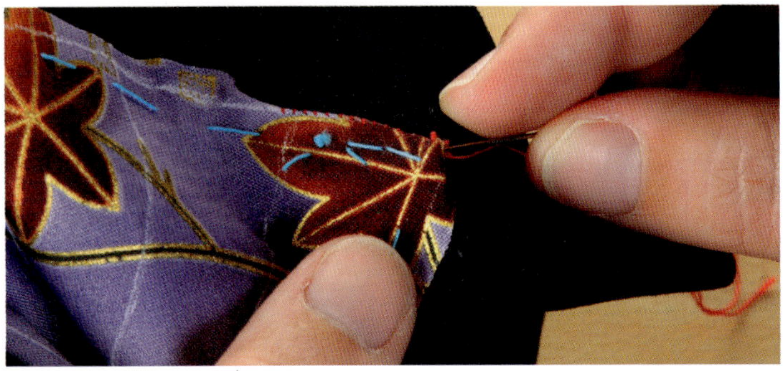

3 Create sharp points and corners by leaving the last couple of stitches loose, pushing the point of the fabric under the shape as far as possible and then gently tightening the sewing thread. The loose stitches will tighten up and the point will pull out perfectly.

Using the templates in the block directory

The templates, kamon crests and takarazukushi symbols in this book need to be enlarged by the specified percentage on a photocopier. Use the enlargement to transfer the pattern onto the background fabric for either sashiko stitching or positioning appliqué pieces (page 41), and then use it to make individual appliqué templates if required. The appliqué method you choose will dictate whether you need to add turning allowances or make paper templates before cutting out each piece of fabric.

Freezer paper appliqué

This method uses paper templates behind the fabric, which is folded and pressed over the paper edge for accuracy. Freezer paper has a waxy side that can be ironed to the back of the fabric, sticking the template in place. Cut out the fabric after ironing on the template, adding a ¼ in. (6 mm) turning allowance all around. After sewing the appliqué shape in place, cut away the background fabric behind it, leaving about a ¼ in. (6 mm) overlap, and gently pull the paper out. If you cannot buy freezer paper, the waxy wrappers from photocopier papers can be substituted.

Fused appliqué

This quick appliqué method involves ironing fusible webbing to the back of the fabric, cutting out the pieces and ironing them onto a backing fabric. Begin by tracing the pattern pieces onto the paper backing of the fusible webbing, remembering to draw a mirror image of the pattern; do not add any turning allowances. Decorate the raw edges with machine satin or embroidery stitches, or simply zigzag with invisible nylon thread. Metallic threads can look like kinkoma (Japanese gold thread embroidery). Note that fusible webbing may stiffen the appliqué motif, making hand sewing difficult.

Fusible bias tape

Ready-made fusible bias tape is easy to use to represent stems, ribbons, branches and so on. It is a Japanese product.

1 Following the manufacturer's instructions, iron the bias tape in place, then sew with small stitches, as for needle-turn appliqué. Where the bias tape overlaps the raw edges of a shape, as here, simply tack the shape and cover the raw edge with the bias tape. Fold under any uncovered ends of tape.

2 Multishaded bias tape is good for overlapping cord effects. Here, the tape ends are tucked under other appliqué edges.

Embroidery details

Accent your appliqué block designs with details in running stitch, stem stitch or French knots.

- Running stitch: Sew a neat line of stitches, with the stitches and spaces between them all equal in length.
- Stem stitch: Bring the needle to the front and then take it to the back to form a long stitch. Bring it to the front again halfway along the stitch just formed. Repeat to sew a line of overlapping stitches of equal length.
- French knots: Bring the needle to the front and wrap the thread around it twice. Keeping the thread taut, take the needle to the back near where it emerged and pull through to leave a knot on the surface.

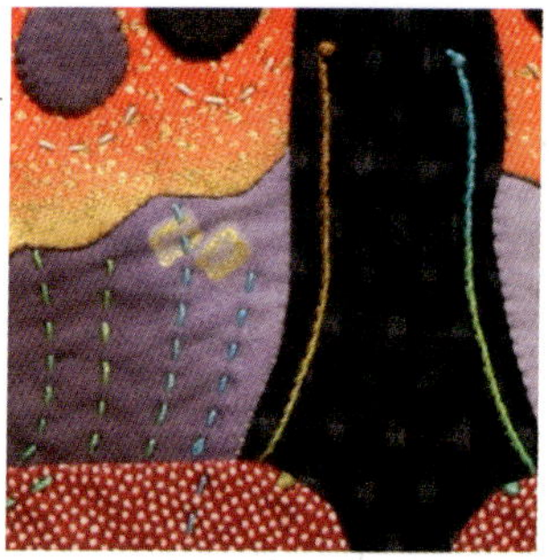

Sashiko

Sashiko fabric needs to have a lower thread count than normal patchwork fabrics or it will be hard to stitch. Fabrics woven specially for sashiko are available in many colours and imitate antique cotton fabric.

Thread

Thread thickness and shade varies between manufacturers, so use the same brand throughout your sashiko project. If you cannot obtain real sashiko thread, cotton à broder makes a reasonable, if expensive, substitute. Cotton perlé does not really look or behave like sashiko thread, although it can add an interesting colour accent. Thread made for sashiko will give you the best results. To use sashiko thread, open out the skein, cut through all the threads at one point and braid them loosely. The threads may seem very long, but do not cut them shorter.

Needles

Select a sashiko needle, a large sharp or a crewel (embroidery) needle – it needs to be sharp, rigid and fairly long. Thread the needle with a whole length of thread and double it. Smooth the thread down, so it does not twist around itself, and tie a single knot at the end so that the thread cannot fall out of the needle if you drop it. A double thread is traditional in sashiko.

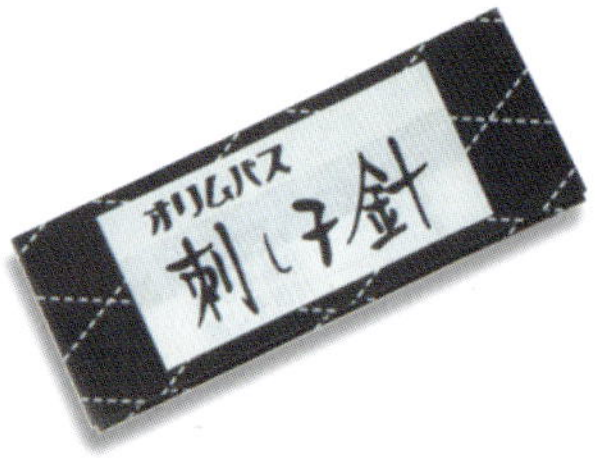

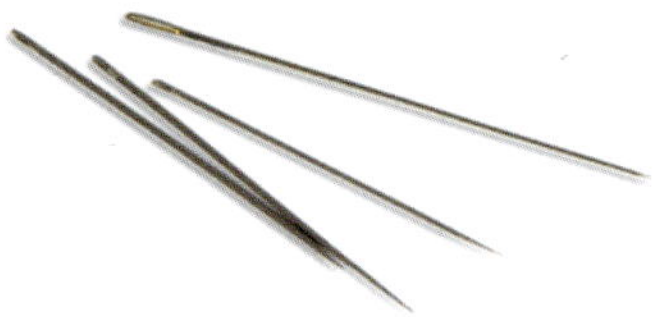

Marking geometric designs

Draw directly on the fabric with a fabric marker – white marking pens, tailor's chalk, soft white watercolour pencils, Nonce pencils, Japanese chaco liners or other light-coloured markers are all suitable.

1 Use the grid on a cutting mat to mark the base grid – the grid size is given with each sashiko block. Make sure you can see the mat grid all around the edge. The ruler should be long enough to reach the opposite sides of the mat.

2 Mark curved lines for patterns like blocks 83 and 90 with an appropriately sized circle template. Use a 1-in. (2.5-cm) diameter coin for tiny circles.

Marking kamon crests and takarazukushi symbols

Use a lightbox, with the pattern under the fabric, or chaco paper (Japanese dressmaker's carbon paper) to transfer these designs. Chaco paper is available in white, yellow, pink and blue. Marks wash out. For both methods, start by enlarging the pattern by the specified percentage on a photocopier.

1 Put the chaco paper face down on the fabric with the pattern on top and pin together. Trace along all the design lines with a ballpoint transfer tool, the end of a knitting needle or something similar.

2 Carefully lift the pattern and chaco paper; the pattern will have transferred onto the fabric. Chaco paper can be reused again and again.

Sashiko stitching tips

- You are aiming for nice, fat running stitches. If your stitches are not even enough, snip off the starting knot, pull out the stitches and start again.
- When turning corners, make the last stitch right into the corner to define the pattern sharply.
- Where pattern lines cross, leave a slightly longer gap between stitches so that stitches do not cross on the right side, making an ugly lump and a weak point in the sashiko. Avoid joining new threads at these points.
- Where pattern lines meet, space the stitches so that they do not touch each other.

Stitching sashiko

Start and finish stitching with a knot on the back. Follow the specified stitching sequence for geometric patterns. For kamon crests and takarazukushi symbols, keep the thread continuous as much as possible, outlining motifs first before filling them in.

1 Pleat the fabric onto the needle, allowing it to gather up as you pull the thread through, then smooth out the stitches. This will make the two strands of thread lie parallel in the stitch, so the stitches look bold and slightly raised on the fabric surface. Keep sewing straight and evenly by making as many stitches as possible with the needle before pulling the thread through. Stitches should be between ⅛ and ¼ in. (3 and 6 mm) long. The gaps between them are about half the length of the stitch. When finished, press lightly from the back.

2 Strand the thread loosely across the back of the work where indicated in the pattern. When you make a sharp change of direction, leave a little loop on the back for ease or the sashiko will pucker.

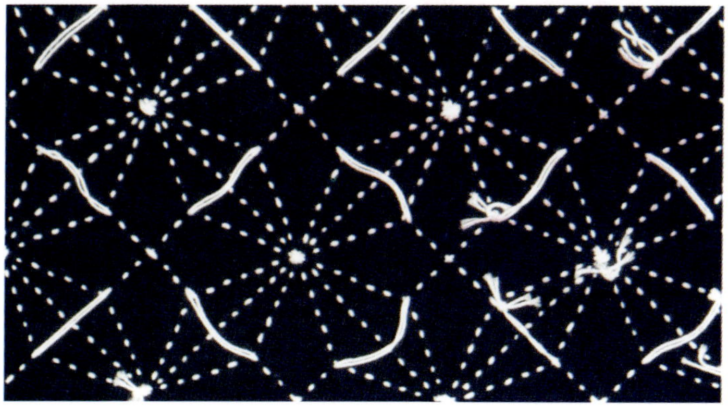

Finishing

Sewing finished blocks together is similar to making a simple patchwork. After pressing the last patchwork seams, sandwich the quilt wadding between the backing and the quilt top, and quilt the whole thing by hand or machine. Finish the quilt with a simple binding.

Borders and sashing

You may wish to add borders or sashing to your quilt. Borders are strips added to blocks individually; sashing is strips sewn between adjacent blocks. This is especially useful for sampler quilts, because it gives unity to a large variety of patterns. An outer border can be added in the same way, taking measurements through the centre of the quilt top rather than along the edge. For borders, the first two borders should be as long as the edges of the block. The next two borders are longer, equalling the block plus the finished width of the first two borders. Pin border strips and sashing in place before sewing. Press seam allowances between blocks in alternate directions.

Sandwiching the layers

The backing and wadding should be about 2 in. (5 cm) larger than the quilt top all around. Press the fabrics and smooth out the backing on a flat, clean surface, covering any important tabletops with heavy cardboard or wooden sheeting. Hold the edges down with masking tape at intervals. Spread the wadding on top and smooth out. Lay the quilt top over the wadding and smooth out, making sure block corners are square. Starting at the centre, tack the layers together. You may wish to pin the layers with dressmaking pins temporarily. Japanese quilters recommend tacking the layers with a diagonal stitch, as shown here, rather than with straight lines of tacking, because it holds the layers more firmly. Use a teaspoon to lever up the point of the needle after each stitch to prevent your fingers from getting sore.

Hand quilting

Many Japanese quilters do not use a quilting frame; with the firm diagonal tacking method used to sandwich the quilt, the layers do not move apart easily. Begin quilting from the centre. Many quilters protect their index fingers with thimbles, one on each hand. To hand quilt, start by tying two knots at the end of the quilting thread. From the front of the quilt, take a long stitch in the opposite direction to the way you will quilt and 'pop' the two knots through the fabric and into the wadding. With your non-sewing hand under the quilt, take small running stitches in a rocking motion, going through all the layers. Feel the needle point emerging under the quilt and immediately push the point up again. Take several stitches at a time before pulling the thread through. At the end, turn the quilt over, tie two more knots and pop these through the backing and into the quilt.

Machine quilting

Machine quilting is more popular in the West than in Japan and has a stronger linear effect than hand quilting. Machine quilting can start and finish at the edge of the quilt, to avoid having lots of loose thread ends to sew in afterwards. Continuous-line patterns are easiest to quilt. Choose toning threads a shade darker than the background fabrics, unless you want a contrast; these samples use red thread for clarity.

1 Use a walking foot on the machine to feed the layers of the quilt sandwich through at the same rate, preventing unsightly puckering. Use it for quilting straight lines 'in the ditch' (in the seam line), parallel lines, grids and gentle curves. With a zigzag throat plate, it can be used to quilt with fancy embroidery stitches on computerized machines.

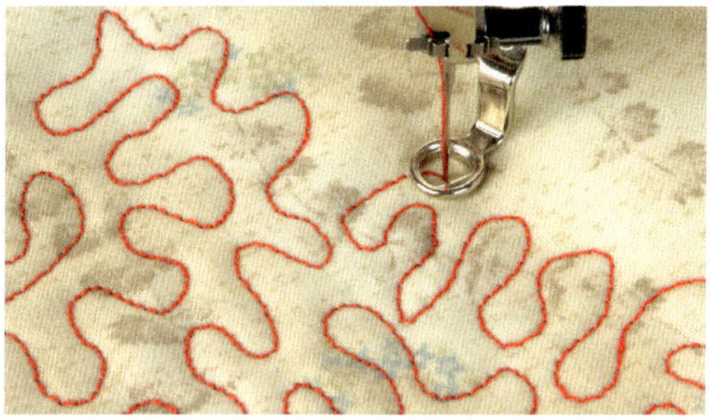

2 Free-motion quilting is done with the machine feed dogs down. You will need a darning, quilting or embroidery foot. Guide the fabric through the machine, moving the quilt in any direction. Move it evenly to maintain a consistent stitch length. Some computerized machines have a movement sensor that regulates the stitching speed for even stitches.

Binding

Trim the backing and wadding to match the edge of the quilt top. Tack or sew all around the top, close to the edge, to hold the layers together. Cut 1½-in. (3.8-mm) wide binding strips, two the same length as the edge to be bound and two 2 in. (5 cm) longer than the remaining edges. Pin the first two strips to the corresponding quilt edges along the front of the quilt, setting the strip edge approximately ¼ in. (6 mm) away from the quilt edge, and sew. Fold the binding around the edge, turn under a ¼ in. (6 mm) allowance and hem by hand with small stitches to the back of the quilt. Repeat for the two remaining edges, but allow the binding to overlap by 1 in. (2.5 cm) at each end when machine sewing. Fold and sew these ends in before hemming the binding to the back.

Finishing tips

- If some blocks are slightly smaller or larger than you expected, add borders or trim so that all the blocks are the same size.
- If you need to join fabric for the quilt backing, use two vertical seams rather than one seam down the centre of the quilt back, where the quilt may be repeatedly folded during its lifetime.
- Some cotton wadding needs to be pre-shrunk unless you want an antique puckered effect the first time you wash the quilt. Pre-shrink it by soaking it in the bathtub in warm water.
- Tacking with safety pins is popular in the West, especially for machine quilting, but take care only to pin through patterned fabrics because the pins can leave tiny holes.
- Decide if you want to bind the top and bottom of the quilt first or the sides – binding the sides second looks better on a bed quilt.
- Cut binding strips on the straight grain for wallhangings; bias-cut binding is better for bed quilts and throws.
- Do not forget to add a signed and dated quilt label; write with an acid-free permanent marker and appliqué the label to the back.

Block Directory

The directory contains photographs and instructions for making more than 125 Japanese quilt blocks, divided into patchwork, sashiko, kamon and takarazukushi designs. Each block is graded by degree of difficulty, so you can choose the ones that suit your own skill level. All of the blocks can be mixed and matched together to create quilts, wallhangings and cushions. Scattered throughout the directory you will find suggestions for mixing and matching the blocks to get you started.

1 Yosegi nikuzushi

(Simple pairs)

CUTTING LIST

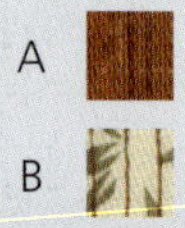

A Four 5 x 3 in. (12.7 x 7.6 cm) strips.
B Eight 5 x 1½ in. (12.7 x 3.8 cm) strips.

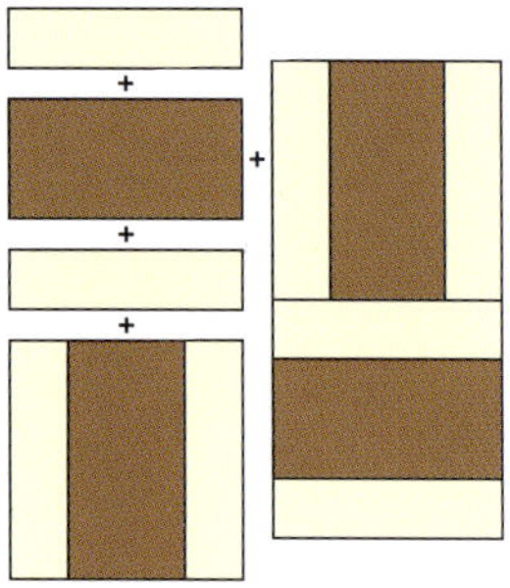

Construction

Sew the block, using the diagram as a guide. The block is assembled in four main pieces.

2 Yosegi gokuzushi

(Simple fives)

Use fabrics with strong colour and tonal contrasts to get the best effect from this block.

CUTTING LIST

A Four 5 x 1⅜ in. (12.7 x 3.5 cm) strips.
B Four 5 x 1⅜ in. (12.7 x 3.5 cm) strips.
C Four 5 x 1⅜ in. (12.7 x 3.5 cm) strips.
D Four 5 x 1⅜ in. (12.7 x 3.5 cm) strips.
E Four 5 x 1½ in. (12.7 x 3.8 cm) strips.

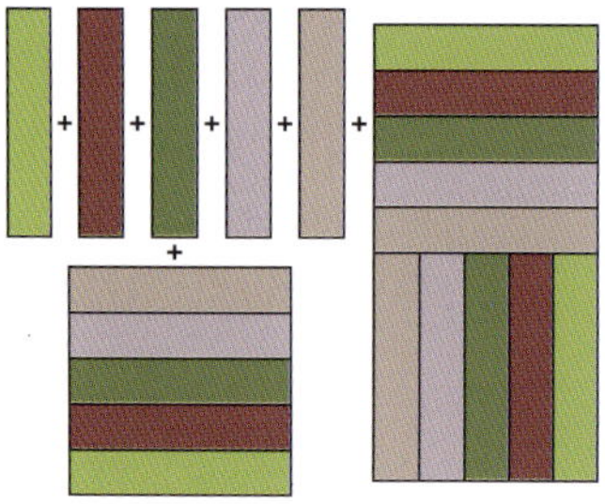

Construction

Sew the block, using the diagram as a guide. The block is assembled in four main pieces.

3 Yosegi kawari nikuzushi

(Simple pairs variation)

Instead of using strips of two different fabrics, you could use a fabric with symmetrical stripes and make the block from nine identical 3½ in. (8.9 cm) squares.

CUTTING LIST

A Eighteen 3½ x 1½ in. (8.9 x 3.8 cm) strips.
B Nine 3½ x 1½ in. (8.9 x 3.8 cm) strips.

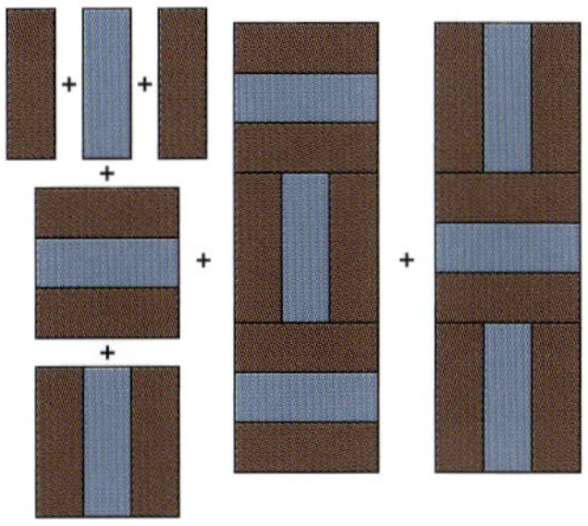

Construction

Sew the block, using the diagram as a guide. The block is assembled in three strips.

4 Hirasan kuzushi

(Simple three lines form)

Use a large-scale print for the big squares.

CUTTING LIST

A Two 5 in. (12.7 cm) squares.
B Eight 2¾ x 1¼ in. (7 x 3.2 cm) strips.
C Eight 2¾ x 1¼ in. (7 x 3.2 cm) strips.
D Eight 2¾ x 1¼ in. (7 x 3.2 cm) strips.

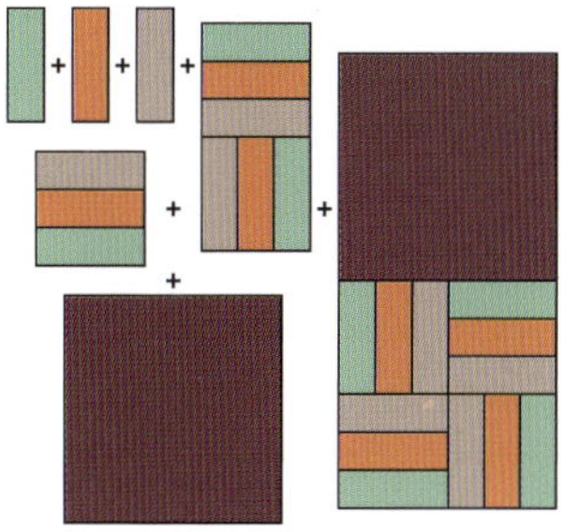

Construction

Sew the block, using the diagram as a guide. The block is assembled in four main pieces.

5 Kurume kasuri igeta

(Kurume well curb)

CUTTING LIST

A
B

- A Nine 2 in. (5 cm) squares.
- A Two 8 x 1¼ in. (20.3 x 3.2 cm) strips.
- A Two 9½ x 1¼ in. (24 x 3.2 cm) strips.
- B Six 2 in. (5 cm) squares.
- B Two 8 x 2 in. (20.3 x 5 cm) strips.

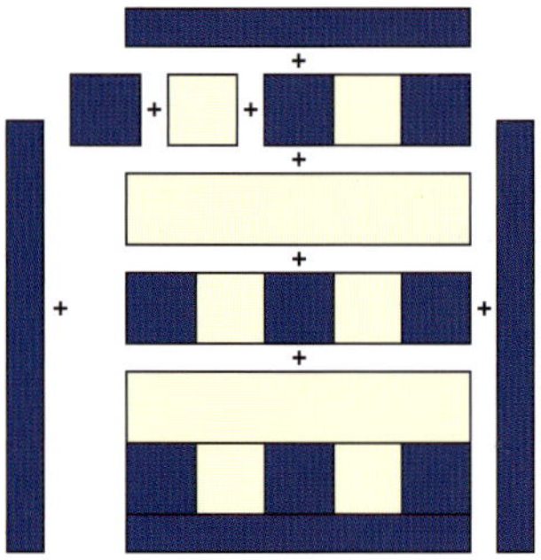

Construction

Sew the block, using the diagram as a guide. The block is assembled in strips.

6 Yamato kasuri igeta

(Yamato well curb)

Fabrics with different-coloured warp and weft threads, such as tsumugi, chambray or shot cotton, enhance the kasuri look.

CUTTING LIST

A
B
C

- A Nine 2 in. (5 cm) squares.
- A Two 8 x 1¼ in. (20.3 x 3.2 cm) strips.
- A Two 9½ x 1¼ in. (24 x 3.2 cm) strips.
- B Twelve 2 in. (5 cm) squares.
- C Four 2 in. (5 cm) squares.

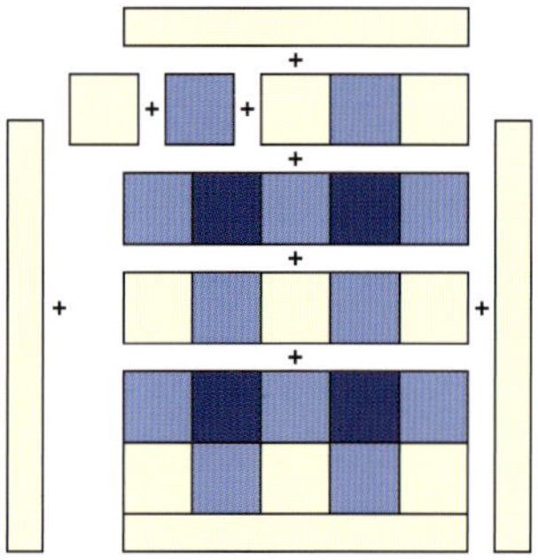

Construction

Sew the block, using the diagram as a guide. The block is assembled in strips.

7 Yamato kasuri igeta jūji

(Yamato well curb cross)

CUTTING LIST

A
B
C

- A Four 3½ x 2 in. (8.9 x 5 cm) strips.
- A Five 2 in. (5 cm) squares.
- A Two 8 x 1¼ in. (20.3 x 3.2 cm) strips.
- A Two 9½ x 1¼ in. (24 x 3.2 cm) strips.
- B Four 2 in. (5 cm) squares.
- B Two 5 x 2 in. (12.7 x 5 cm) strips.
- C Two 2 in. (5 cm) squares.

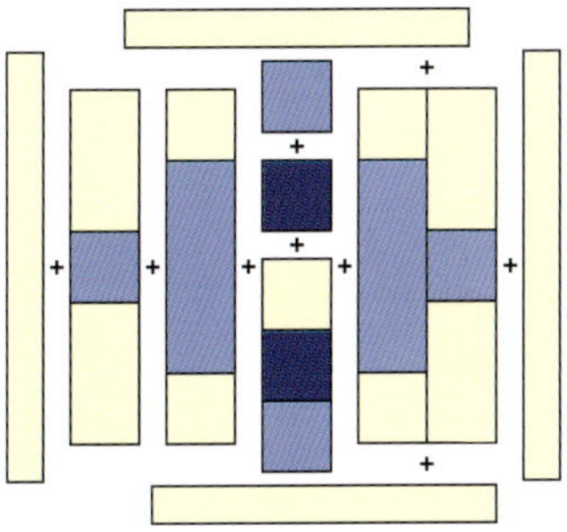

Construction

Sew the block, using the diagram as a guide. The block is assembled in strips.

8 Meisen hana

(Meisen silk flower)

CUTTING LIST

A
B
C
D

- A Four 3½ x 2 in. (8.9 x 5 cm) strips.
- A Four 2 in. (5 cm) squares.
- A Two 8 x 1¼ in. (20.3 x 3.2 cm) strips.
- A Two 9½ x 1¼ in. (24 x 3.2 cm) strips.
- B Eight 2 in. (5 cm) squares.
- C Four 2 in. (5 cm) squares.
- D One 2 in. (5 cm) square.

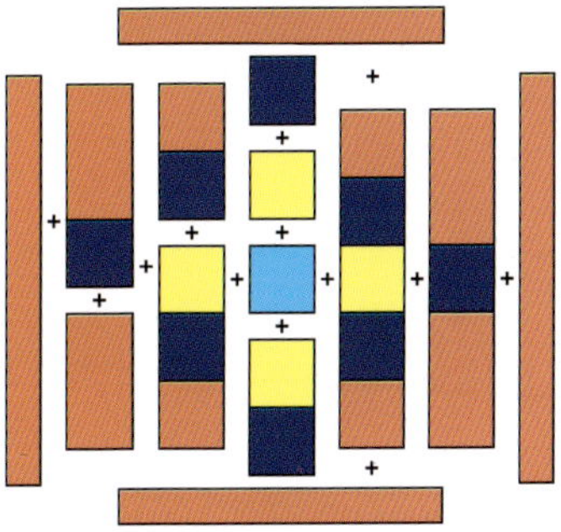

Construction

Sew the block, using the diagram as a guide. The block is assembled in strips.

9 Kurume kasuri tōfu mon

(White square pattern)

CUTTING LIST

A Eight 2 in. (5 cm) squares.
A Two 8 x 1¼ in. (20.3 x 3.2 cm) strips.
A Two 9½ x 1¼ in. (24 x 3.2 cm) strips.
B Four 3½ x 2 in. (8.9 x 5 cm) strips.
B Two 5 x 2 in. (12.7 x 5 cm) strips.
B Three 2 in. (5 cm) squares.

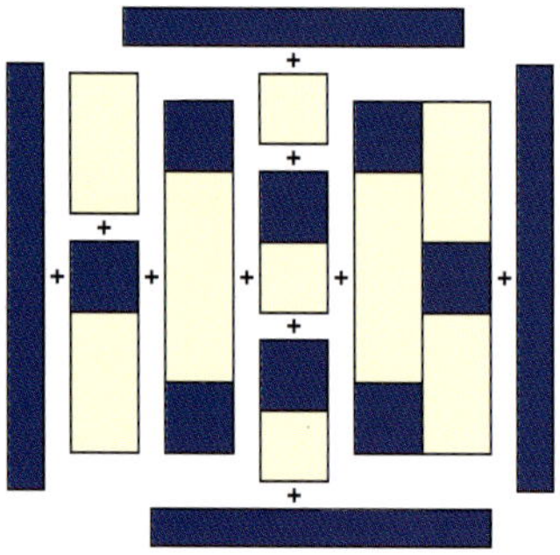

Construction

Sew the block, using the diagram as a guide. The block is assembled in strips.

10 Kurume kasuri kumitate ichimatsu

(One-square check structure)

CUTTING LIST

A Four 5½ x 2½ in. (14 x 6.4 cm) strips.
A Four 3½ x 1½ in. (8.9 x 3.8 cm) strips.
A Four 1½ in. (3.8 cm) squares.
B Two 2½ in. (6.4 cm) squares.
C Nine 1½ in. (3.8 cm) squares.
C Two 2½ in. (6.4 cm) squares.

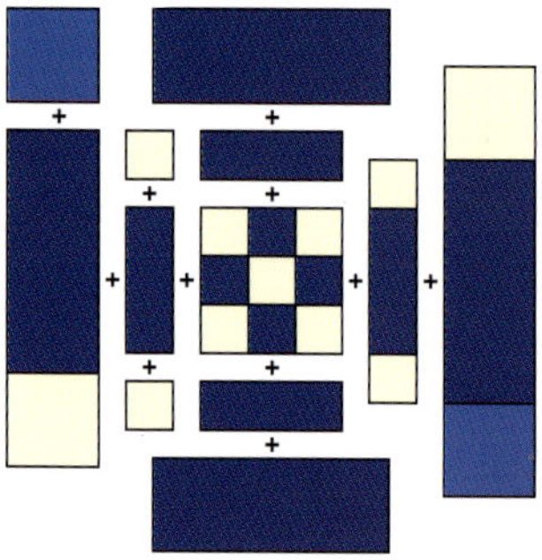

Construction

Sew the block, using the diagram as a guide. The block is assembled from the centre outwards.

11 Kurume kasuri igeta jūji

(Kurume well curb cross)

CUTTING LIST

A One 2½ in. (6.4 cm) square.
A Four 1½ in. (3.8 cm) squares.
A Four 2½ x 1½ in. (6.4 x 3.8 cm) strips.
A Two 8½ x 1 in. (21.6 x 2.5 cm) strips.
A Two 9½ x 1 in. (24 x 2.5 cm) strips.
B Four 2½ in. (6.4 cm) squares.
C Four 2½ in. (6.4 cm) squares.
C Eight 2½ x 1½ in. (6.4 x 3.8 cm) strips.

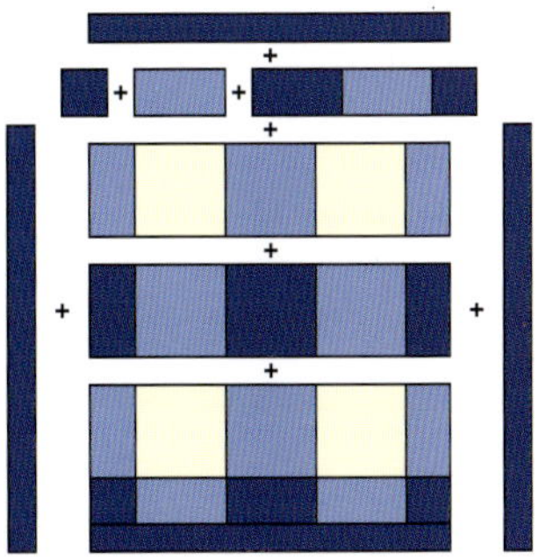

Construction

Sew the block, using the diagram as a guide. The block is assembled in strips.

12 Yosegi jūji masu

(Cross squares)

CUTTING LIST

A Eight 2 in. (5 cm) squares.
A Two 3½ x 2 in. (8.9 x 5 cm) strips.
A One 3½ x 6 in. (8.9 x 15.2 cm) strip.
B Eight 2 in. (5 cm) squares.
B Four 3½ x 2 in. (8.9 x 5 cm) strips.

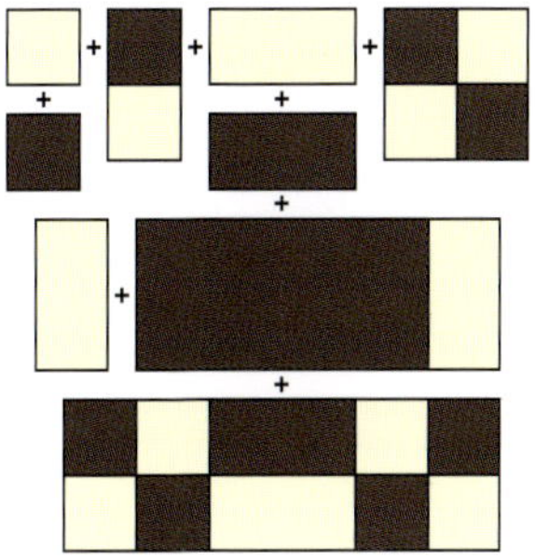

Construction

Sew the block, using the diagram as a guide. The block is assembled in strips.

13 Yosegi kōshi tsunagi

(Linked check)

CUTTING LIST

A
B

- A One 5½ in. (14 cm) square.
- A Eight 1½ in. (3.8 cm) squares.
- A Eight 3 x 1½ in. (7.6 x 3.8 cm) strips.
- B Eight 1½ in. (3.8 cm) squares.
- B Eight 3 x 1½ in. (7.6 x 3.8 cm) strips.

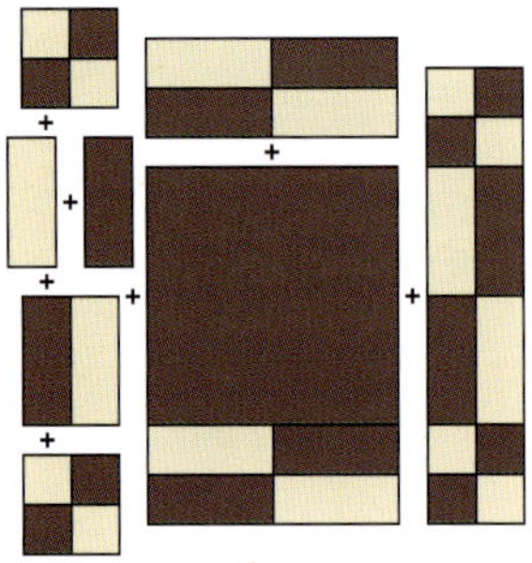

Construction

Sew the block, using the diagram as a guide. The block is assembled in strips.

14 Kurume kasuri musubi

(Knot)

CUTTING LIST

A
B
C

- A Five 1½ in. (3.8 cm) squares.
- A Four 2½ x 1½ in. (6.4 x 3.8 cm) strips.
- A Two 7½ x 1½ in. (19 x 3.8 cm) strips.
- A Two 9½ x 1½ in. (24 x 3.8 cm) strips.
- B Six 1½ in. (3.8 cm) squares.
- B Four 3½ x 1½ in. (8.9 x 3.8 cm) strips.
- C Two 5½ x 1½ in. (14 x 3.8 cm) strips.
- C Four 2½ x 1½ in. (6.4 x 3.8 cm) strips.

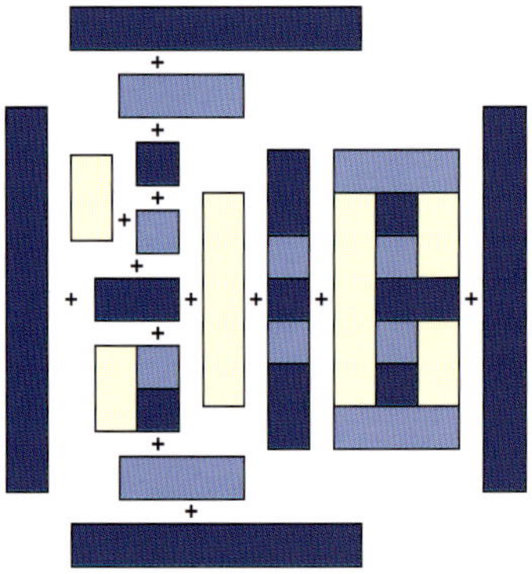

Construction

Sew the block, using the diagram as a guide. Make the knot 'loops' first. The block is assembled in strips.

15 Kurume kasuri tsunagi masumon

(Linked square pattern)

CUTTING LIST

A	A	Four 2½ in. (6.4 cm) squares.
	A	Nine 1½ in. (3.8 cm) squares.
	A	Four 2½ x 1½ in. (6.4 x 3.8 cm) strips.
B	B	Four 4½ x 1½ in. (11.4 x 3.8 cm) strips.
	B	Eight 3½ x 1½ in. (8.9 x 3.8 cm) strips.
	B	Four 2½ x 1½ in. (6.4 x 3.8 cm) strips.

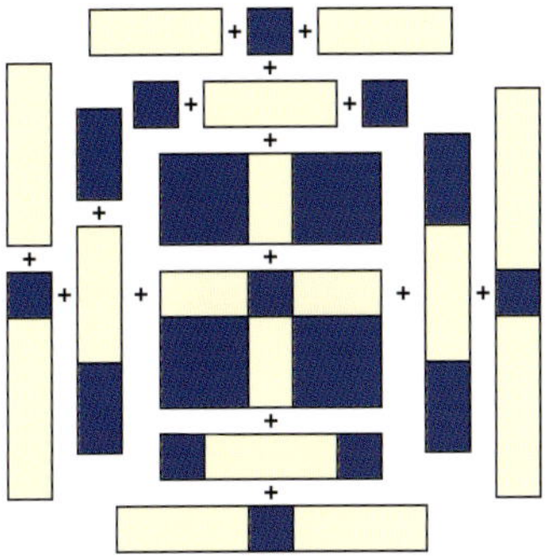

Construction

Sew the block, using the diagram as a guide. Assemble the centre in strips, then complete the block from the centre outwards.

Mix & Match

ideas for combining blocks

Above, from top left: 6 each x blocks 34 (alternate blocks rotated 90 degrees), 13, 57, 1, 27 and 3 (alternate blocks rotated 90 degrees). Below, from centre out: 5 x block 22; 4 x block 32; 16 x block 2; 24 x block 25.

16 Kurume kasuri masu tsunagi

(Linked squares)

CUTTING LIST

A Five 1½ in. (3.8 cm) squares.
A Four 3½ x 1½ in. (8.9 x 3.8 cm) strips.
A Sixteen 2½ x 1½ in. (6.4 x 3.8 cm) strips.
B Twenty-six 1½ in. (3.8 cm) squares.
B Two 3½ x 1½ in. (8.9 x 3.8 cm) strips.

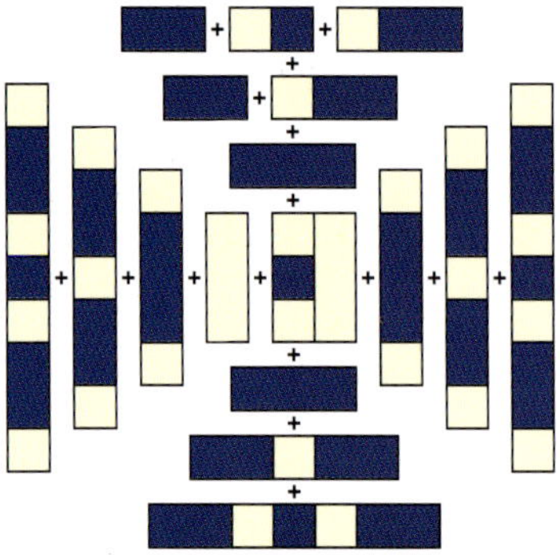

Construction

Sew the block, using the diagram as a guide. The block is assembled from the centre outwards.

17 Kurume kasuri gakubuchi

(Frame)

CUTTING LIST

A One 5½ in. (14 cm) square.
A Four 1½ in. (3.8 cm) squares.
A Four 3½ x 1½ in. (8.9 x 3.8 cm) strips.
B Four 5½ x 1½ in. (14 x 3.8 cm) strips.
B Four 3½ x 1½ in. (8.9 x 3.8 cm) strips.
B Four 2½ x 1½ in. (6.4 x 3.8 cm) strips.

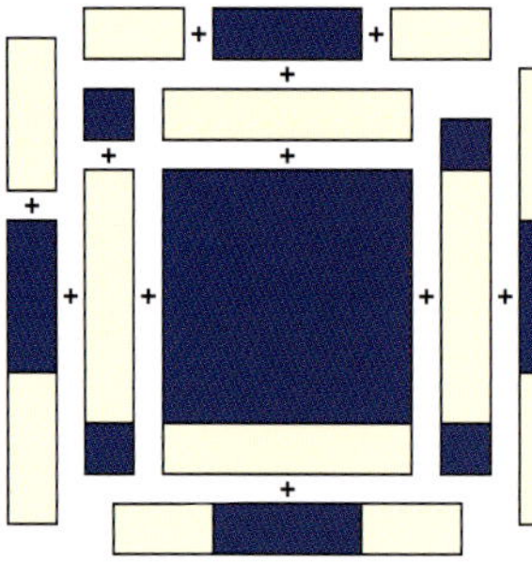

Construction

Sew the block, using the diagram as a guide. The block is assembled from the centre outwards.

18 Kurume kasuri masumon

(Kurume square pattern)

CUTTING LIST

A Two 3½ in. (8.9 cm) squares.
A Two 5½ x 3½ in. (14 x 8.9 cm) strips.
A Eight 1½ in. (3.8 cm) squares.
A Four 3½ x 1½ in. (8.9 x 3.8 cm) strips.
B One 3½ in. (8.9 cm) square.
C Four 1½ in. (3.8 cm) squares.

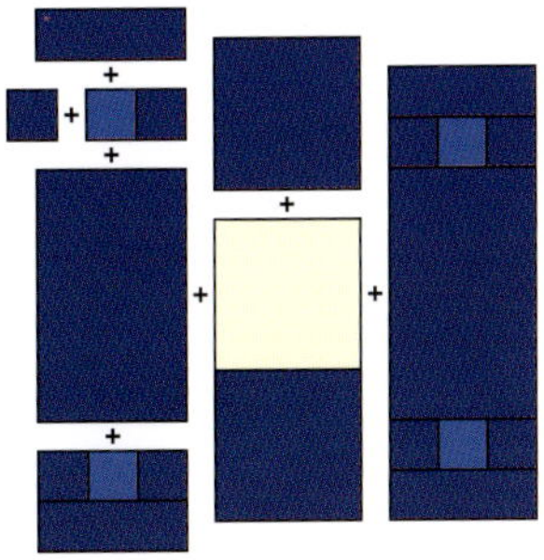

Construction

Sew the block, using the diagram as a guide. The block is assembled in strips.

19 Kurume kasuri sanju masu

(Triple squares)

CUTTING LIST

A One 1½ in. (3.8 cm) square.
A Two 2½ x 1 in. (6.4 x 2.5 cm) strips.
A Two 3½ x 1 in. (8.9 x 2.5 cm) strips.
A Two 5½ x 1 in. (14 x 2.5 cm) strips.
A Two 6½ x 1 in. (16.5 x 2.5 cm) strips.
B Four 1 in. (2.5 cm) squares.
B Four 1½ in. (3.8 cm) squares.
B Four 2 in. (5 cm) squares.
C Four 1½ x 1 in. (3.8 cm x 2.5 cm) strips.
C Four 3½ x 1½ in. (8.9 x 3.8 cm) strips.
C Four 6½ x 2 in. (16.5 x 5 cm) strips.

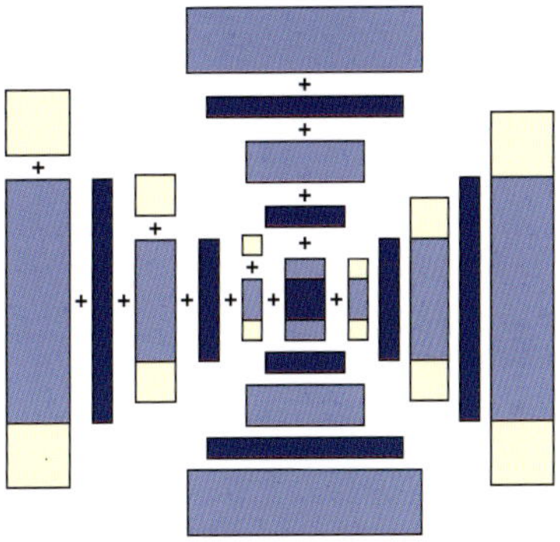

Construction

Sew the block, using the diagram as a guide. The block is assembled from the centre outwards.

20 Kurume kasuri haba ni masumon

(Two-width square pattern)

CUTTING LIST

A — B — C

- A Four 1½ in. (3.8 cm) squares.
- A Two 4½ in. (11.4 cm) squares.
- A Two 8½ x 1 in. (21.6 x 2.5 cm) strips.
- A Two 9½ x 1 in. (24 x 2.5 cm) strips.
- B Two 1½ in. (3.8 cm) squares.
- B Two 2½ x 1½ in. (6.4 x 3.8 cm) strips.
- B Two 4½ x 1½ in. (11.4 x 3.8 cm) strips.
- C Two 1½ in. (3.8 cm) squares.
- C Two 2½ x 1½ in. (6.4 x 3.8 cm) strips.
- C Two 4½ x 1½ in. (11.4 x 3.8 cm) strips.

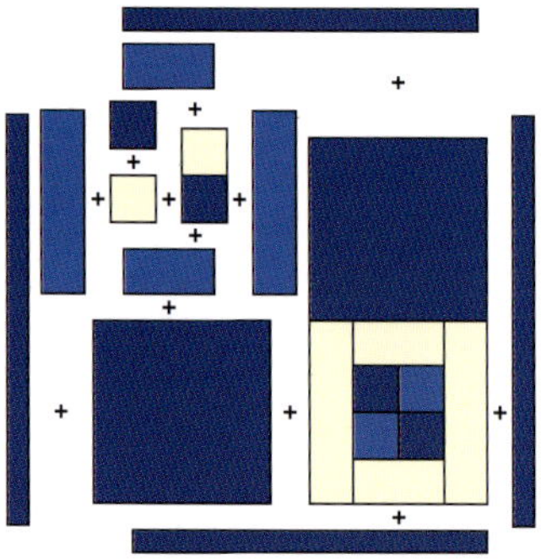

Construction

Sew the block, using the diagram as a guide. The block is assembled in four sections, then the border is added.

21 Meisen igeta

(Meisen silk well curbs)

CUTTING LIST

A — B — C

- A Two 4¼ in. (10.8 cm) squares.
- A Eighteen 1¼ in. (3.2 cm) squares.
- A Two 8 x 1¼ in. (20.3 x 3.2 cm) strips.
- A Two 9½ x 1¼ in. (24 x 3.2 cm) strips.
- B Two 4¼ x 1¼ in. (10.8 x 3.2 cm) strips.
- B Six 1¼ in. (3.2 cm) squares.
- C Two 4¼ x 1¼ in. (10.8 x 3.2 cm) strips.
- C Six 1¼ in. (3.2 cm) squares.

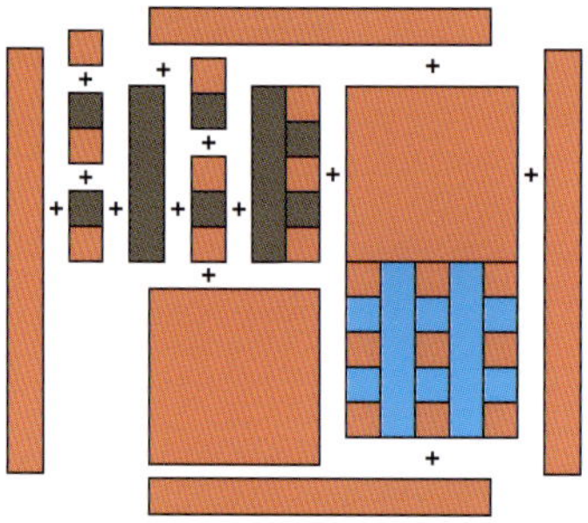

Construction

Sew the block, using the diagram as a guide. The block is assembled in strips, starting with the checked quarters.

22 Tsumeta

(Boxed rice fields)

CUTTING LIST

A Sixteen 1½ in. (3.8 cm) squares.
B Eight 2½ x 1¼ in. (6.4 x 3.2 cm) strips.
B Eight 4 x 1¼ in. (10.2 x 3.2 cm) strips.
C Two 4 x 1 in. (10.2 x 2.5 cm) strips.
C One 8 x 1 in. (20.3 x 2.5 cm) strip.
C Two 8 x 1¼ in. (20.3 x 3.2 cm) strips.
C Two 9½ x 1¼ in. (24 x 3.2 cm) strips.

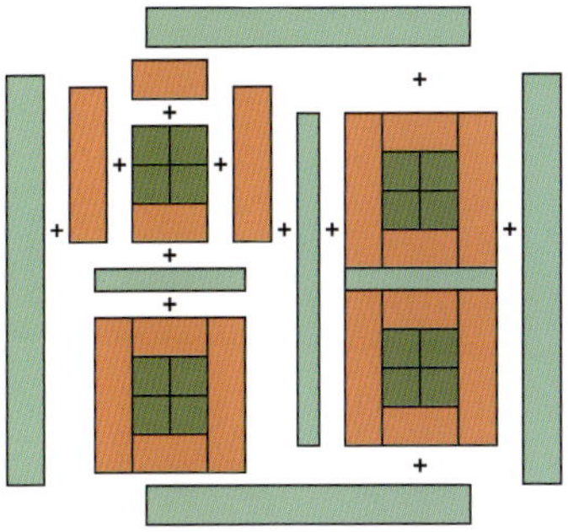

Construction

Sew the block, using the diagram as a guide. The block is assembled in four sections, then in strips and finally the border is added.

23 Kurume kasuri goku masu

(Five squares)

CUTTING LIST

A Two 5½ x 1½ in. (14 x 3.8 cm) strips.
A Two 3½ x 1½ in. (8.9 x 3.8 cm) strips.
B One 1½ in. (3.8 cm) square.
B Two 7½ x 1½ in. (19 x 3.8 cm) strips.
B Two 5½ x 1½ in. (14 x 3.8 cm) strips.
C Two 1½ in. (3.8 cm) squares.
C Two 3½ x 1½ in. (8.9 x 3.8 cm) strips.
C Two 9½ x 1½ in. (24 x 3.8 cm) strips.
C Two 7½ x 1½ in. (19 x 3.8 cm) strips.

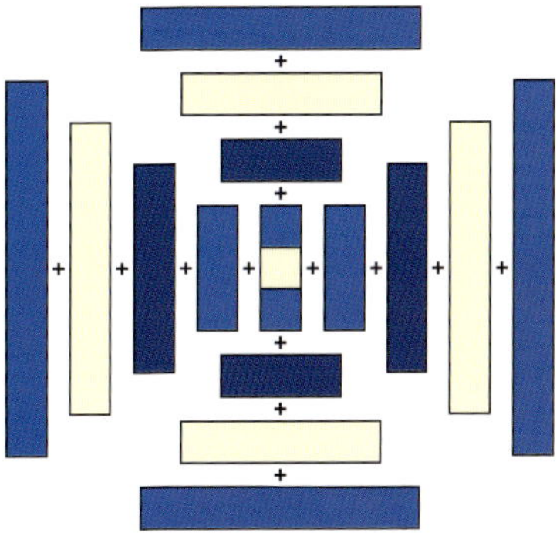

Construction

Sew the block, using the diagram as a guide. The block is assembled from the centre outwards.

24 Hiratsume sanmasu

(Three concentric squares)

CUTTING LIST

A
B

- A Two 1½ in. (3.8 cm) squares.
- A Two 3½ x 1½ in. (8.9 x 3.8 cm) strips.
- A Two 4½ x 1½ in. (11.4 x 3.8 cm) strips.
- A Two 6½ x 1½ in. (16.5 x 3.8 cm) strips.
- A Two 7½ x 1½ in. (19 x 3.8 cm) strips.
- A Two 9½ x 1½ in. (24 x 3.8 cm) strips.
- B One 1½ in. (3.8 cm) square.
- B Two 3½ x 1 in. (8.9 x 3.8 cm) strips.
- B Two 4½ x 1 in. (11.4 x 2.5 cm) strips.
- B Two 6½ x 1 in. (16.5 x 2.5 cm) strips.
- B Two 7½ x 1 in. (19 x 2.5 cm) strips.

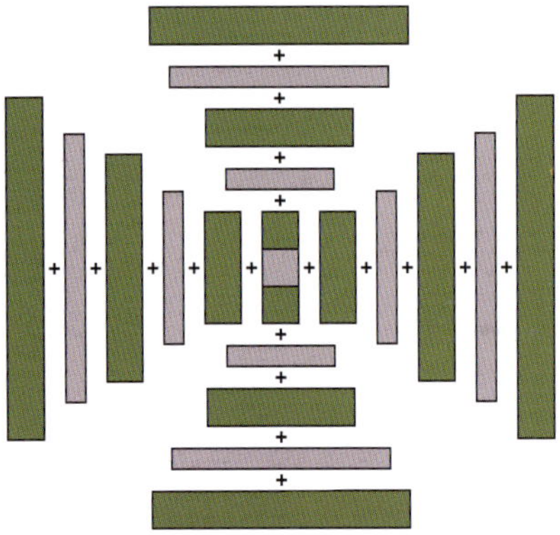

Construction

Sew the block, using the diagram as a guide. The block is assembled from the centre outwards.

25 Pieced raimon

(Spiral)

CUTTING LIST

A
B

- A Two 1½ x 1 in. (3.8 x 2.5 cm) strips.
- A Two 2½ x 1 in. (6.4 x 2.5 cm) strips.
- A Two 3½ x 1 in. (8.9 x 2.5 cm) strips.
- A Two 4½ x 1 in. (11.4 x 2.5 cm) strips.
- A Two 5½ x 1 in. (14 x 2.5 cm) strips.
- A Two 6½ x 1 in. (16.5 x 2.5 cm) strips.
- A Two 7½ x 1 in. (19 x 2.5 cm) strips.
- A Two 8½ x 1 in. (21.6 x 2.5 cm) strips.
- A One 9½ x 1 in. (24 x 2.5 cm) strip.
- B Cut all the above again in this fabric.

Construction

Sew the block, using the diagram as a guide. The block is assembled from the centre outwards.

26 Yosegi kaku to sankaku

(Squares and triangles)

CUTTING LIST

A Two 5 in. (12.7 cm) squares.
A Two 2 in. (5 cm) squares.
B Two 5 in. (12.7 cm) squares.
C Two 2 in. (5 cm) squares.

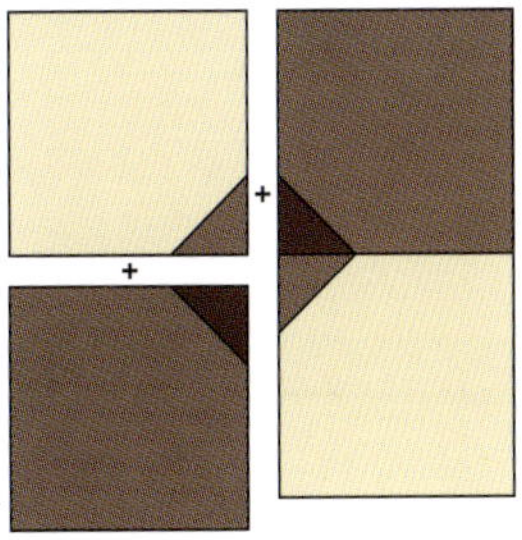

Construction

Sew the block, using the diagram as a guide. Sew the corner triangles using the fast corners method (page 37). The block is assembled in four main pieces.

27 Yosegi hakkakkei to sankaku

(Octagons and triangles)

CUTTING LIST

A Two 5 in. (12.7 cm) squares.
A Eight 2 in. (5 cm) squares.
B Two 5 in. (12.7 cm) squares.
C Eight 2 in. (5 cm) squares.

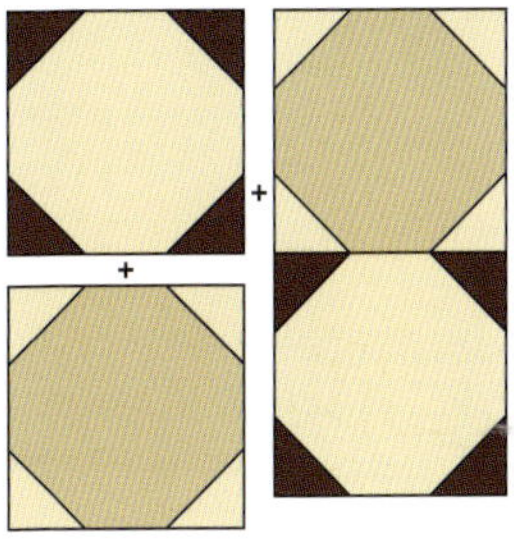

Construction

Sew the block, using the diagram as a guide. Sew the octagons with corner triangles using the fast corners method (page 37). The block is assembled in four main peces.

28 Yosegi kōshi kumitate

(Check frame)

CUTTING LIST

A
B
C
D
E

- A Sixteen 1½ in. (3.8 cm) squares.
- B Sixteen 1½ in. (3.8 cm) squares.
- B Eight 3½ x 1½ in. (8.9 x 3.8 cm) strips.
- C Four 1½ in. (3.8 cm) squares.
- C Four 3½ x 1½ in. (8.9 x 3.8 cm) strips.
- D One 3⅞ in. (9.8 cm) square.
- E One 3⅞ in. (9.8 cm) square.

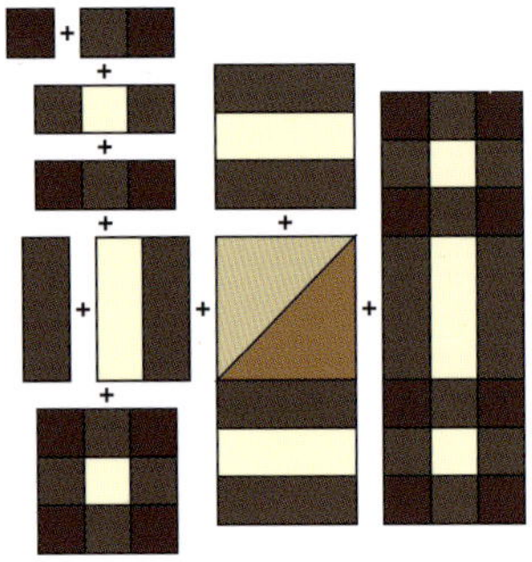

Construction

Sew the block, using the diagram as a guide. Sew D and E to make the central square using the triangle square method (page 36). The block is assembled in three strips. Use the spare triangle square for another block.

29 Uroko

(Scales)

CUTTING LIST

A
B
C

- A Seven 3 in. (7.6 cm) squares.
- B Two 4¼ in. (10.8 cm) squares, cut in quarters diagonally.
- B Two 2⅜ in. (6 cm) squares, cut in half diagonally.
- C Seven 3 in. (7.6 cm) squares.

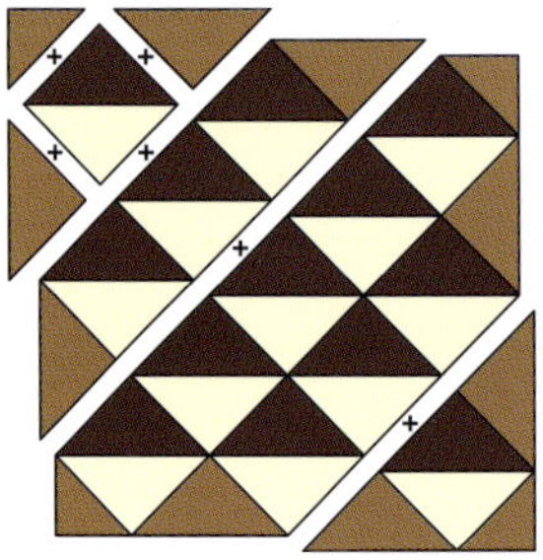

Construction

Sew the block, using the diagram as a guide. Sew pairs of A and C squares together using the triangle square method (page 36). The block is assembled in diagonal strips. Use the spare triangle square for another block.

30 Jūjitsunagi

(Linked '10' variation)

CUTTING LIST

A
B
C

- A Eighteen 1½ in. (3.8 cm) squares.
- A Six 3½ x 1½ in. (8.9 x 3.8 cm) strips.
- A Two 2½ x 1½ in. (6.4 x 3.8 cm) strips.
- B Eight 1½ in. (3.8 cm) squares.
- B Three 3½ x 1½ in. (8.9 x 3.8 cm) strips.
- B Two 2½ x 1½ in. (6.4 x 3.8 cm) strips.
- C Eight 1½ in. (3.8 cm) squares.
- C Four 3½ x 1½ in. (8.9 x 3.8 cm) strips.

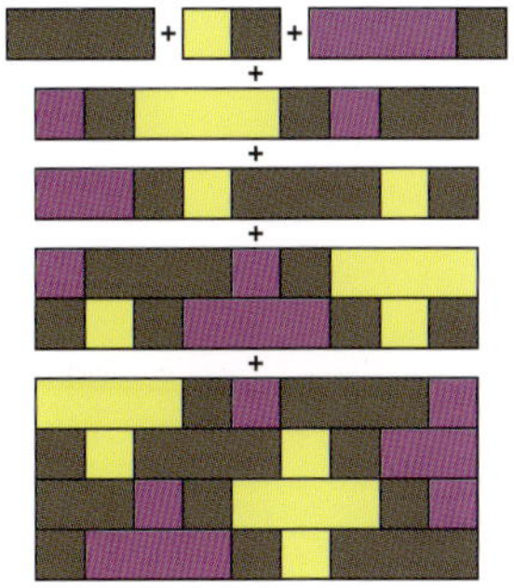

Construction

Sew the block, using the diagram as a guide. The block is assembled in strips.

Mix & Match

ideas for combining blocks

Above, from top left: 25 x block 28; 24 x block 55.
Below, from top left: 25 x block 38; 24 x block 30.

31 Igeta ni hakkaku tsunagi

(Special linked well curbs)

CUTTING LIST

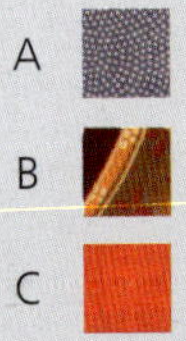

- A Twenty-eight 1½ in. (3.8 cm) squares.
- A Three 3½ x 1½ in. (8.9 x 3.8 cm) strips.
- A Six 2½ x 1½ in. (6.4 x 3.8 cm) strips.
- B Four 3½ in. (8.9 cm) squares.
- C Twelve 1½ in. (3.8 cm) squares.

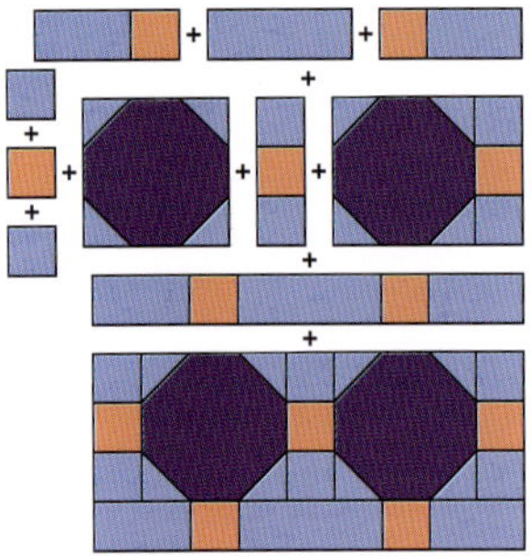

Construction

Sew the block, using the diagram as a guide. Sew the octagons with corner triangles using the fast corners method (page 37). The block is assembled in strips.

32 Zeni

(Coin)

CUTTING LIST

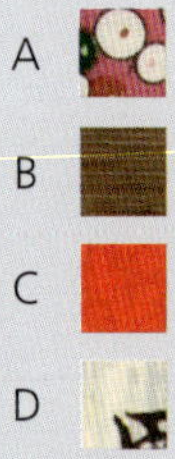

- A Twelve 1½ in. (3.8 cm) squares.
- A Eight 1½ x 2½ in. (3.8 x 6.4 cm) strips.
- A Four 1½ x 3½ in. (3.8 x 8.9 cm) strips.
- B Eight 1½ in. (3.8 cm) squares.
- B Eight 1½ x 3½ in. (3.8 x 8.9 cm) strips.
- C Twelve 1½ in. (3.8 cm) squares.
- D Thirteen 1½ in. (3.8 cm) squares.

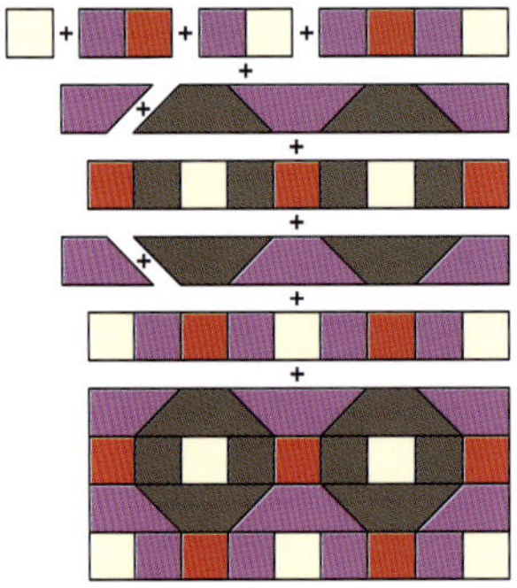

Construction

Sew the block, using the diagram as a guide. Join the strips of A and B in rows using the sewing mitres method (page 35). The block is assembled in strips.

33 Manji

(Buddhist symbol)

Signifying life and the universe, manji is an ancient Buddhist symbol from India.

CUTTING LIST

A B C D E

A Two 3⅞ in. (9.8 cm) squares.
A One 4¼ in. (10.8 cm) square.
B One 3⅞ in. (9.8 cm) square.
B One 4¼ in. (10.8 cm) square.
C One 3⅞ in. (9.8 cm) square.
C One 4¼ in. (10.8 cm) square.
D One 3⅞ in. (9.8 cm) square.
D One 4¼ in. (10.8 cm) square.
E One 3⅞ in. (9.8 cm) square.
E One 4¼ in. (10.8 cm) square.
Cut the smaller squares in half diagonally.
Cut the larger squares in quarters diagonally.

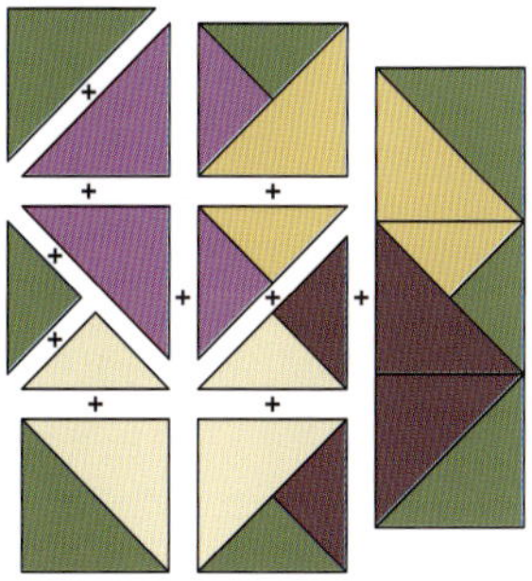

Construction

Sew the block, using the diagram as a guide. Take care not to stretch the bias edges as you sew. The block is assembled in strips. One large and one small triangle of B, C, D and E will be left over, so use these for another block.

34 Yosegi kakudo

(Angles)

CUTTING LIST

A B C D

A One 6¼ in. (15.9 cm) square.
B One 6¼ in. (15.9 cm) square.
C Two 10¼ x 2½ in. (26 x 6.4 cm) strips.
D Two 10¼ x 2½ in. (26 x 6.4 cm) strips.
Cut the squares in quarters diagonally.
Cut a 45-degree triangle from each end of the strips to make trapezoids measuring 5¾ in. (14.6 cm) along the shorter sides.

Construction

Sew the block, using the diagram as a guide. Take care not to stretch the bias edges as you sew. Two A and B triangles will be left over, so use these to make another block.

35 Yosegi nijū kazaguruma

(Double pinwheel)

CUTTING LIST

A Two 3⅜ in. (8.6 cm) squares.
A Two 8¼ x 2½ in. (21 x 6.4 cm) strips.
B Two 3⅜ in. (8.6 cm) squares.
C Two 8¼ x 2½ in. (21 x 6.4 cm) strips.
Cut the squares in half diagonally.
Cut the strips in half along a 45-degree line to make quadrangles measuring 5⅜ in. (13.7 cm) along the longest edge and 3⅛ in. (7.9 cm) along the opposite edge. Cut A with the 45-degree angle slanting to the right and C with the slant to the left.

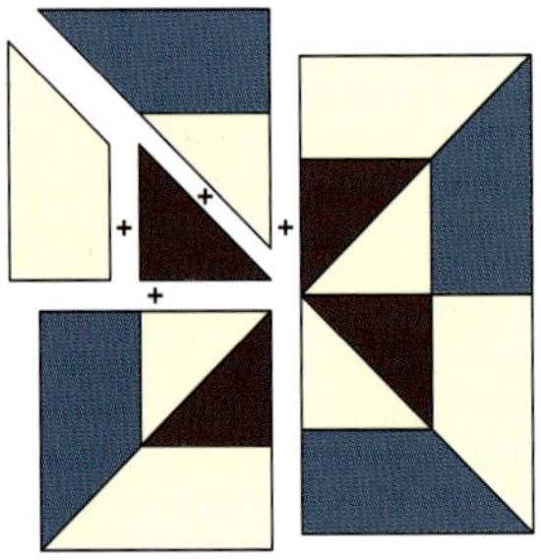

Construction

Sew the block, using the diagram as a guide. Take care not to stretch the bias edges as you sew.

36 Yosegi ichimatsu masu

(Checks and squares)

Cut the triangles from a long piece of striped fabric, fitting the shapes together to get the most out of the design. Match the stripes in sets of four triangles.

CUTTING LIST

A Eight right-angled triangles, 2⅞ in. (7.3 cm) high at centre and 5¾ in. (14.6 cm) wide at base.
B Ten 1½ in. (3.8 cm) squares.
B Eight 1½ x 1¼ in. (3.8 x 3.2 cm) strips.
B Eight 1¼ in. (3.2 cm) squares.
C Eight 1½ in. (3.8 cm) squares.
C Sixteen 1½ x 1¼ in. (3.8 x 3.2 cm) strips.

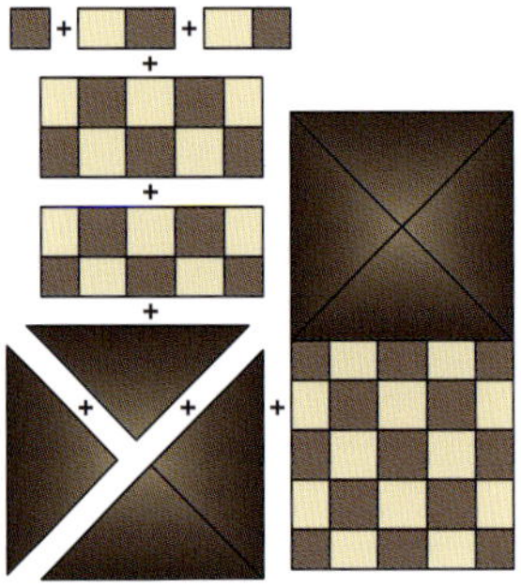

Construction

Sew the block, using the diagram as a guide. Take care not to stretch the bias edges as you sew. The strips and smaller squares go at the outer edges of the chequerboard sections. The block is assembled in four main pieces.

37 Tatami

(Rice straw mats)

Use a large-scale print fabric to emphasize the patchwork seams.

CUTTING LIST

A Eight 2½ x 4½ in. (6.4 x 11.4 cm) strips.
B Two 9½ x 1 in. (24 x 2.5 cm) strips.
B Two 8½ x 1 in. (21.6 x 2.5 cm) strips.

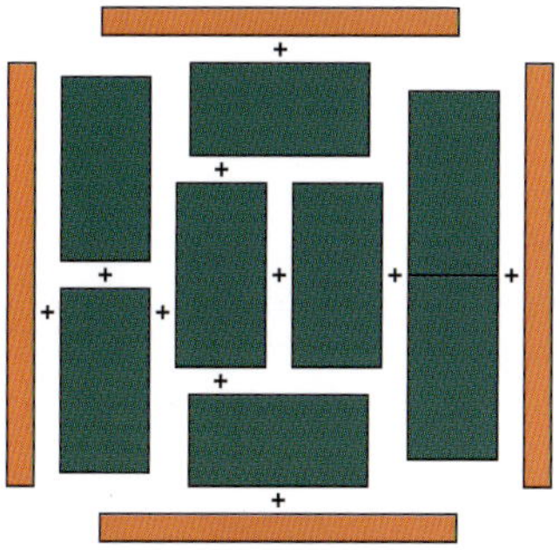

Construction

Sew the block, using the diagram as a guide. The block is assembled from the centre outwards.

38 Irori

(Sunken hearth)

This block is good for directional prints and stripes.

CUTTING LIST

A Four 6½ x 3½ in. (16.5 x 8.9 cm) strips.
B One 3½ in. (8.9 cm) square.

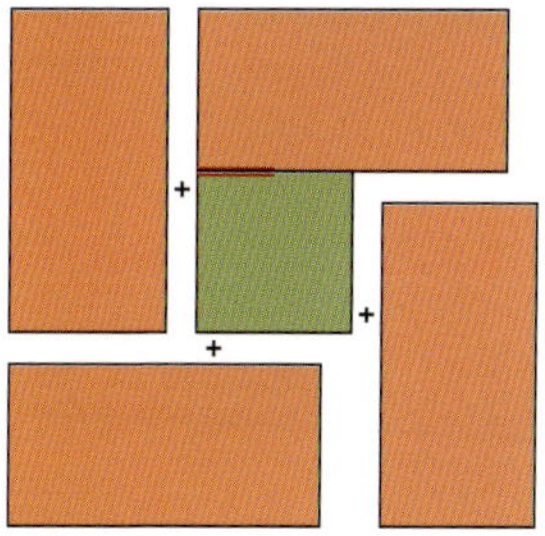

Construction

Sew the block, using the diagram as a guide. The block is assembled from the centre outwards. Begin with the seam shown in red, following the part-sewn seams method (page 35).

39 Kirichigae

(Changed cut)

To get the best effect, cut the strips from a long piece of striped fabric so that the stripes are the same on each one, then arrange the triangles to create a kaleidoscope pattern.

CUTTING LIST

- A Eight 5½ x 2½ in. (14 x 6.4 cm) strips, cut in half diagonally so that the diagonal line slopes in the same direction each time.
- B Four 2¾ in. (7 cm) squares.

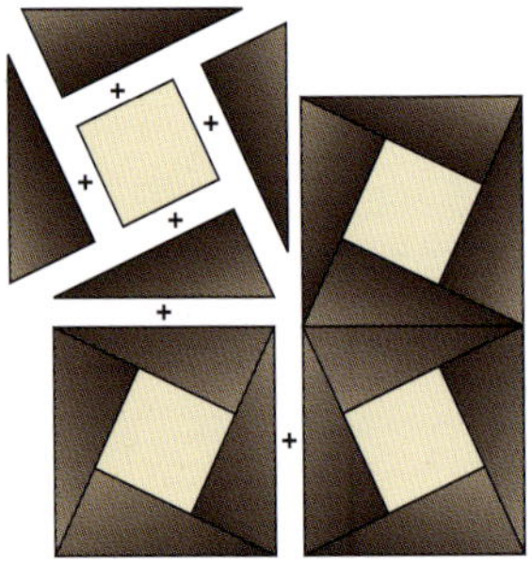

Construction

Sew the block, using the diagram as a guide. Follow the assembly method for block 38 for each section. Take care not to stretch the bias edges as you sew. The block is assembled in four main pieces.

40 Iyo kasuri tsunagi masumon

(Linked squares pattern)

Choose a striped fabric for the border to enhance the design.

CUTTING LIST

- A Two 2½ in. (6.4 cm) squares.
- A Two 4½ x 2½ in. (11.4 x 6.4 cm) strips.
- B Three 2½ in. (6.4 cm) squares.
- C Four 8 x 2 in. (20.3 x 2 cm) strips.

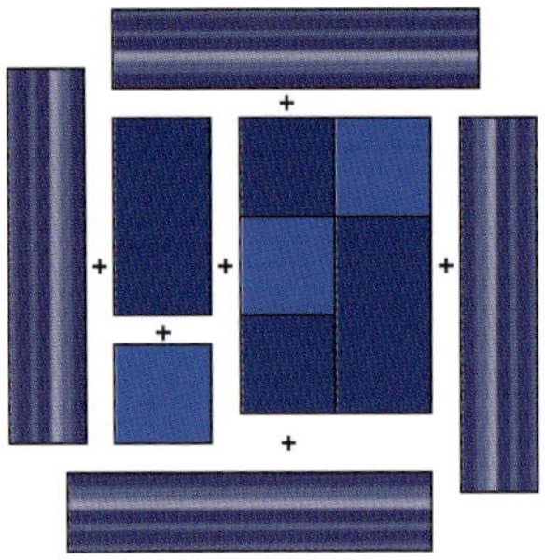

Construction

Sew the block, using the diagram as a guide. The centre of the block is assembled in three strips. Follow the assembly method for block 38 to add the border strips.

41 Meisen kōshi

(Meisen silk check)

Use sixteen different-coloured fabrics for the squares, and arrange the squares so that the colours graduate harmoniously from one tone to another.

CUTTING LIST

A
B

- A Two 8 x 1¼ in. (20.3 x 3.2 cm) strips.
- A Two 9½ x 1¼ in. (24 x 3.2 cm) strips.
- A Three 8 x 1 in. (20.3 x 2.5 cm) strips.
- A Twelve 2 x 1 in. (5 x 2.5 cm) strips.
- B Sixteen 2 in. (5 cm) squares in different colours.

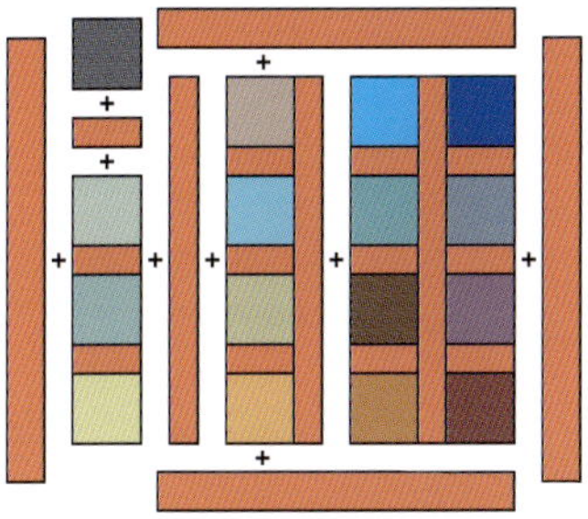

Construction

Sew the block, using the diagram as a guide. The block is assembled in strips.

42 Iyo kasuri masumon

(Iyo square pattern)

CUTTING LIST

A
B
C
D

- A Five 1½ in. (3.8 cm) squares.
- A Four 3 x 2½ in. (7.6 x 6.4 cm) strips.
- A Two 8½ x 1 in. (21.6 x 2.5 cm) strips.
- A Two 9½ x 1 in. (24 x 2.5 cm) strips.
- B Two 1½ x 1 in. (3.8 x 2.5 cm) strips.
- B Two 2½ x 1 in. (6.4 x 2.5 cm) strips.
- C Ten 2½ x 1 in. (6.4 x 2.5 cm) strips.
- C Four 3½ x 1 in. (8.9 x 2.5 cm) strips.
- C Two 8½ x 1 in. (21.6 x 2.5 cm) strips.
- D Eight 1½ x 1 in. (3.8 x 2.5 cm) strips.
- D Eight 2½ x 1 in. (6.4 x 2.5 cm) strips.

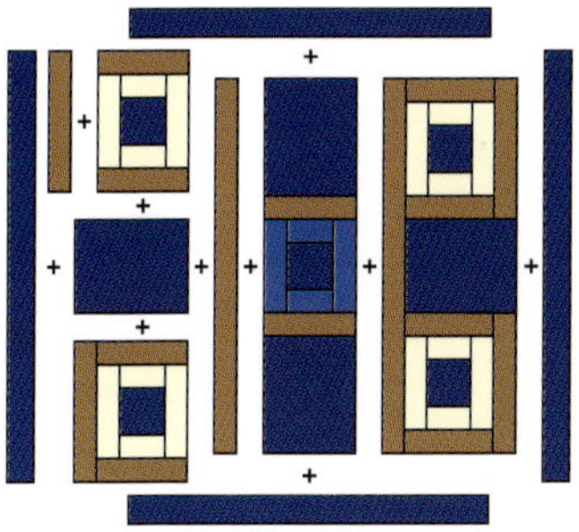

Construction

Sew the block, using the diagram as a guide. The block is assembled in strips. Assemble the squares in the knot in the same way as the squares in block 43.

43 Iyo kasuri komochi masumon

(Iyo 'parent and child' squares)

CUTTING LIST

A
B
C

- A Four 1½ in. (3.8 cm) squares.
- A Twelve 2½ x 1½ in. (6.4 x 3.8 cm) strips.
- A Two 7½ x 1½ in. (19 x 3.8 cm) strips.
- A Two 9½ x 1½ in. (24 x 3.8 cm) strips.
- B Eight 1½ x 1 in. (3.8 x 2.5 cm) strips.
- C Nine 1½ in. (3.8 cm) squares.
- C Eight 2½ x 1 in. (6.4 x 2.5 cm) strips.

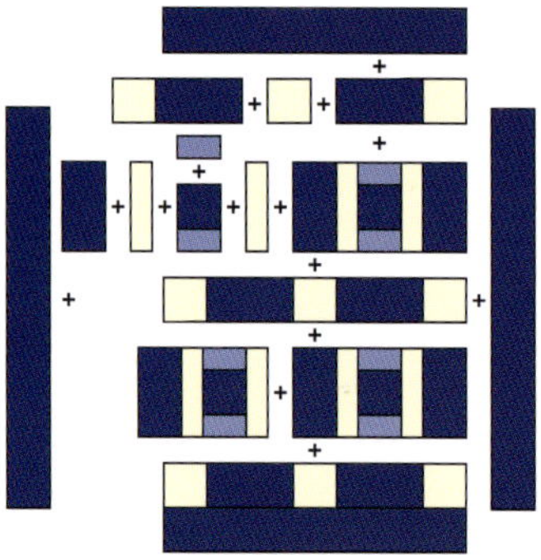

Construction

Sew the block, using the diagram as a guide. The block is assembled in strips.

44 Kurume kasuri kago jūji kika

(Geometric caged cross)

CUTTING LIST

A
B
C

- A Four 1 in. (2.5 cm) squares.
- A Four 2 in. (5 cm) squares.
- A Four 3½ x 2 in. (8.9 x 5 cm) strips.
- A Two 8 x 1¼ in. (20.3 x 3.2 cm) strips.
- A Two 9½ x 1¼ in. (24 x 3.2 cm) strips.
- B Four 2 in. (5 cm) squares.
- C Five 1 in. (2.5 cm) squares.
- C Eight 2 in. (5 cm) squares.

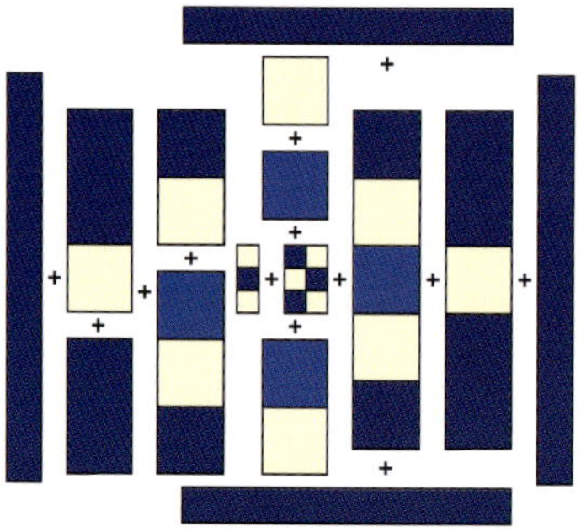

Construction

Sew the block, using the diagram as a guide. The block is assembled in strips.

45 Kurume kasuri fukumoji

(Good luck character)

CUTTING LIST

A
B

- A Four 1 in. (2.5 cm) squares.
- A One 2 x 1 in. (5 x 2.5 cm) strip.
- A Four 3 x 1 in. (7.6 x 2.5 cm) strips.
- A Two 4 x 1 in. (10.2 x 2.5 cm) strips.
- A One 6 x 1 in. (15.2 x 2.5 cm) strip.
- A Two 6 x 2¼ in. (15.2 x 5.7 cm) strips.
- A Two 9½ x 2¼ in. (24 x 5.7 cm) strips.
- B Two 1 in. (2.5 cm) squares.
- B Seven 2 x 1 in. (5 x 2.5 cm) strips.
- B Five 3 x 1 in. (7.6 x 2.5 cm) strips.
- B Three 4 x 1 in. (10.2 x 2.5 cm) strips.

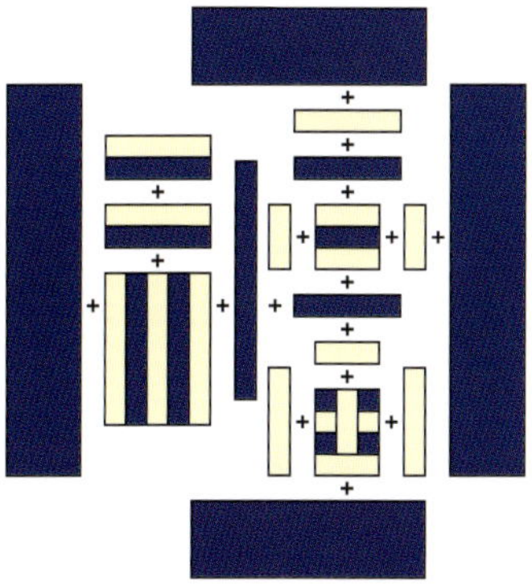

Construction

Sew the block, using the diagram as a guide. The block is assembled in sections.

Mix & Match

ideas for combining blocks

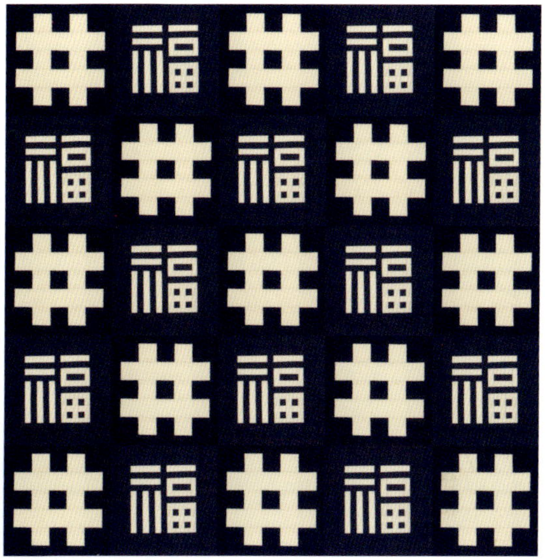

Above, from top left: 13 x block 5; 12 x block 45.
Below, from top left: 25 x block 17; 24 x block 44.

46 Meisen maru

(Meisen silk circle)

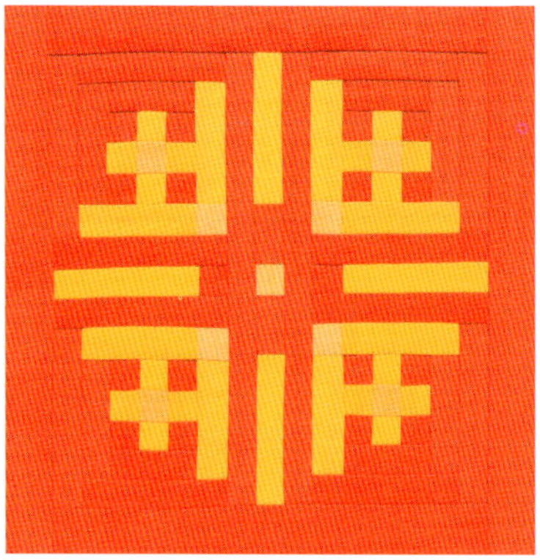

CUTTING LIST

A, B, C

- A Two 8 x 1¼ in. (20.3 x 3.2 cm) strips.
- A Two 9½ x 1¼ in. (24 x 3.2 cm) strips.
- A Eighteen 1 in. (2.5 cm) squares.
- A Four 1 x 2 in. (2.5 x 5 cm) strips.
- A Four 1 x 2½ in. (2.5 x 6.4 cm) strips.
- A Four 1 x 3 in. (2.5 x 7.6 cm) strips.
- A Eight 1 x 3½ in. (2.5 x 8.9 cm) strips.
- A Two 1 x 8 in. (2.5 x 20.3 cm) strips.
- A Two 1 x 1½ in. (2.5 x 3.8 cm) strips.
- B Sixteen 1 in. (2.5 cm) squares.
- B Eight 1 x 2½ in. (2.5 x 6.4 cm) strips.
- B Four 1 x 3 in. (2.5 x 7.6 cm) strips.
- C Nine 1 in. (2.5 cm) squares.

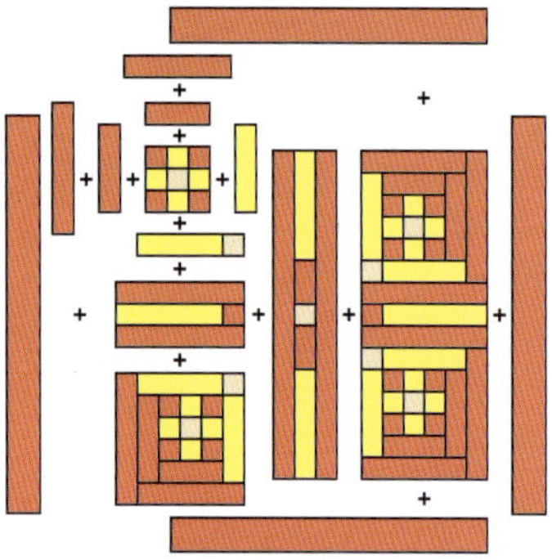

Construction

Sew the block, using the diagram as a guide. The block is assembled in strips.

47 Tatemimasu

(Three upright squares)

Use small-scale prints to create the illusion of solid layered squares. For a perfect 9 in. (22.8 cm) block, take slightly generous seams when piecing the squares and triangles together.

CUTTING LIST

A, B, C, D

- A One 3¾ in. (9.5 cm) square.
- A Two 4⅛ in. (10.5 cm) squares, cut in half diagonally.
- A One 4½ in. (11.4) square, cut in quarters diagonally.
- B Eight 1 x 3¾ in. (2.5 x 9.5 cm) strips.
- B Eight 1 x 2¾ in. (2.5 x 7 cm) strips.
- C Eight 1 x 2¾ in. (2.5 x 7 cm) strips.
- C Eight 1 x 1¾ in. (2.5 x 4.4 cm) strips.
- D Four 1¾ in. (4.4 cm) squares.

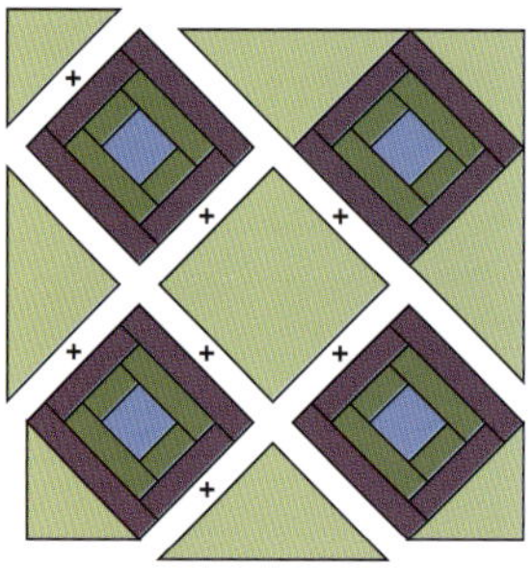

Construction

Sew the block, using the diagram as a guide. Follow the assembly method for block 23 for the layered squares. The block is assembled in diagonal strips.

48 Kumiko

(Lattice)

Use striped fabric to create a spinning effect. For a perfect 9 in. (22.8 cm) block, take slightly generous seams when piecing the squares and triangles together.

CUTTING LIST

A 
B 
C 
D 

A One 3¾ in. (9.5 cm) square.
A Two 4⅛ in. (10.5 cm) squares, cut in half diagonally.
A One 4½ in. (11.4 cm) square, cut in quarters diagonally.
B Sixteen 1 x 3¼ in. (8.3 cm) strips.
C Sixteen 1 x 2¼ in. (5.7 cm) strips.
D Four 1¾ in. (4.4 cm) squares.

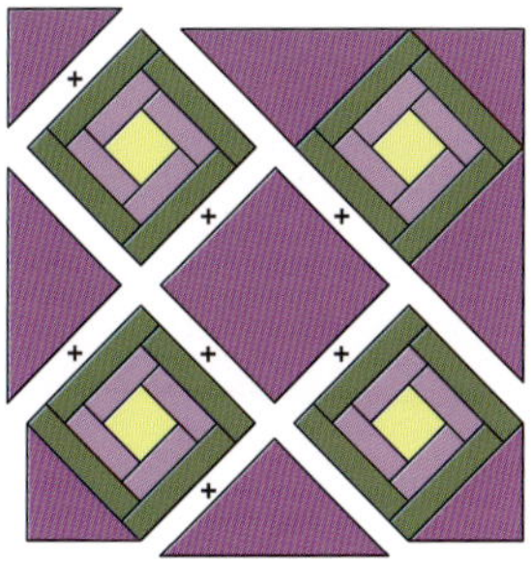

Construction

Sew the block, using the diagram as a guide. Follow the assembly method for block 38 for the layered squares. The block is assembled in diagonal strips.

49 Yosegi kawari royagoshi

(Prison grille check variation)

Use striped fabric to emphasize the weave effect.

CUTTING LIST

A 
B 
C 

A Four 6 x 2 in. (15.2 x 5 cm) strips.
A Four 2½ x 2 in. (6.4 x 5 cm) strips.
B Eighteen 1½ in. (3.8 cm) squares.
C Eighteen 1½ in. (3.8 cm) squares.

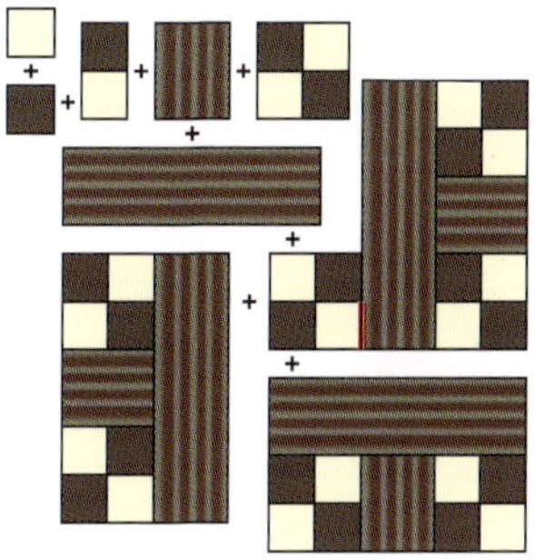

Construction

Sew the block, using the diagram as a guide. Complete the outer sections first, then assemble the block from the centre outwards. Begin with the seam shown in red, using the part-sewn seams method (page 35).

50 Yosegi kawari royagoshi no.2

(Prison grille check variation no.2)

Use a landscape print for the squares to suggest a view beyond the lattice.

CUTTING LIST

- A Ten 2½ x 1½ in. (6.4 x 3.8 cm) strips.
- A Fifteen 3½ x 1½ in. (8.9 x 3.8 cm) strips.
- B Sixteen 1½ in. (3.8 cm) squares.

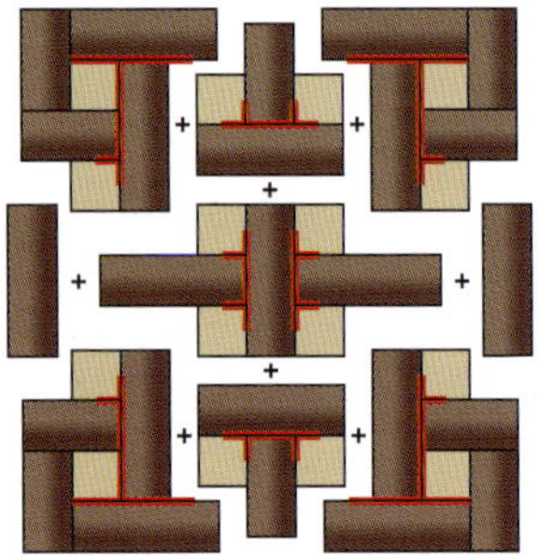

Construction

Sew the block, using the diagram as a guide and the part-sewn seams method (page 35). Assemble the block into the sections shown, then sew these together, again with part-sewn seams, to complete the block.

51 Pieced sayagata

(Saya brocade pattern)

Making the four-patch units from the same striped fabric as the strips, matched to the adjacent stripe colour, creates the illusion of the sayagata design in patchwork, but it needs careful planning and uses a lot of fabric. For a simpler version, use a two-colour stripe.

CUTTING LIST

- A Eight 4 x 2 in. (10.2 x 5 cm) strips.
- A Eight 3 x 2 in. (7.6 x 5 cm) strips.
- A Thirty-six 1 in. (2.5 cm) squares.

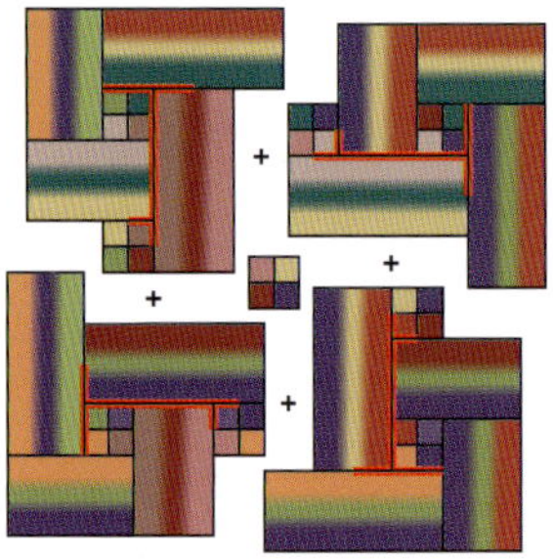

Construction

Sew the block, using the diagram as a guide and the part-sewn seams method (page 35). Make the four-patch units first. Assemble the block into the sections shown, then sew these together, again with part-sewn seams, to complete the block.

52 Yosegi higaki

(Cypress fence)

Striped or directional fabrics will accentuate the woven effect.

CUTTING LIST

A Two 3½ x 2 in. (8.9 x 5 cm) strips.
A Two 2 in. (5 cm) squares.
B Three 3½ x 2 in. (8.9 x 5 cm) strips.
B One 2 in. (5 cm) square.
C Five 3½ x 2 in. (8.9 x 5 cm) strips.
C One 2 in. (5 cm) square.
D Four 3½ x 2 in. (8.9 x 5 cm) strips.
D One 2 in. (5 cm) square.
E One 3½ x 2 in. (8.9 x 5 cm) strip.
E One 2 in. (5 cm) square.

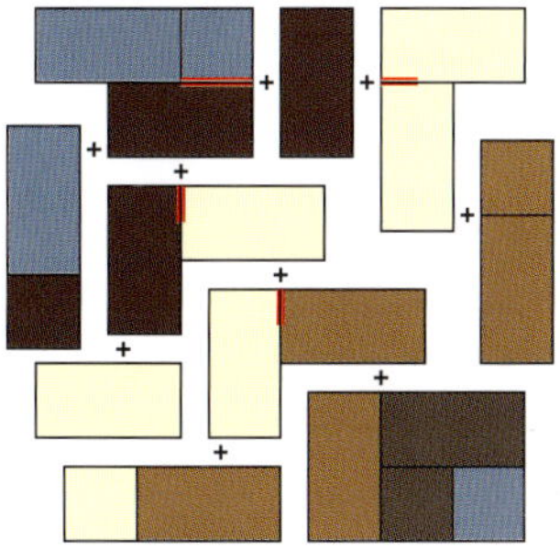

Construction

Sew the block, using the diagram as a guide and the part-sewn seams method (page 35). Assemble the block into the sections shown, then sew these together starting at the top left, again with part-sewn seams, to complete the block.

53 Yosegi kawari higaki

(Cypress fence variation)

Accentuate the woven effect by using striped or directional fabrics.

CUTTING LIST

A Two 2¼ in. (5.7 cm) squares, cut in half diagonally.
A One 2⅝ in. (6.7 cm) square, cut in quarters diagonally.
A Two 1⅞ x 3¼ in. (4.8 x 8.3 cm) strips.
B Four 1⅞ x 3¼ in. (4.8 x 8.3 cm) strips.
B One 2¼ in. (5.7 cm) square, cut in half diagonally.
C Cut the same pieces as B.
D Cut the same pieces as B.
E Cut the same pieces as B.
F Two ¾ x 9 in. (1.9 x 22.8 cm) strips.
F Two ¾ x 9½ in. (1.9 x 24 cm) strips.
Cut a 45-degree triangle from the right end of both A strips and two of the E strips so that the angle slants down to the right.

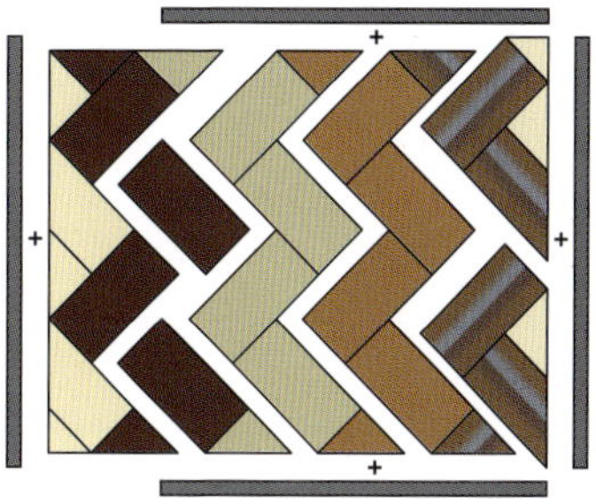

Construction

Sew the block, using the diagram as a guide and the assembly method for block 52. Add the border strips last. Two small A corner triangles will be left over, so use these for another block.

54 Yosegi chūshin no jūji

(Central cross)

CUTTING LIST

A Four 2½ in. (6.4 cm) squares.
B Four 2½ x 1½ in. (6.4 x 3.8 cm) strips.
C One 1½ in. (3.8 cm) square.
D Four 10¼ x 2½ in. (26 x 6.4 cm) strips.
Cut a 45-degree triangle from each end of the D strips to make trapezoids measuring 5¾ in. (14.6 cm) along the shorter sides.

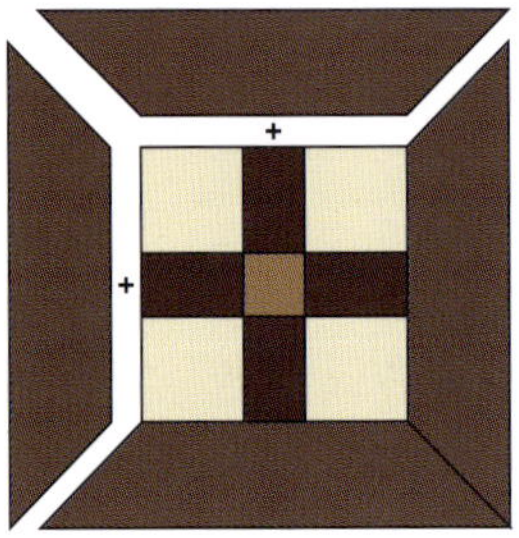

Construction

Sew the block, using the diagram as a guide. Assemble the centre first, then add the trapezoids, following the tips on inset seams (page 34).

55 Yosegi naname jūji

(Diagonal cross)

Cut four B strips following the stripe and four on the bias for an interesting effect.

CUTTING LIST

A One 7¼ in. (18.4 cm) square, cut in quarters diagonally.
B Eight 7½ x 1½ in. (19 x 3.8 cm) strips.
Cut a 45-degree triangle from each end of the strips to make trapezoids measuring 4½ in. (11.4 cm) along the shorter sides.

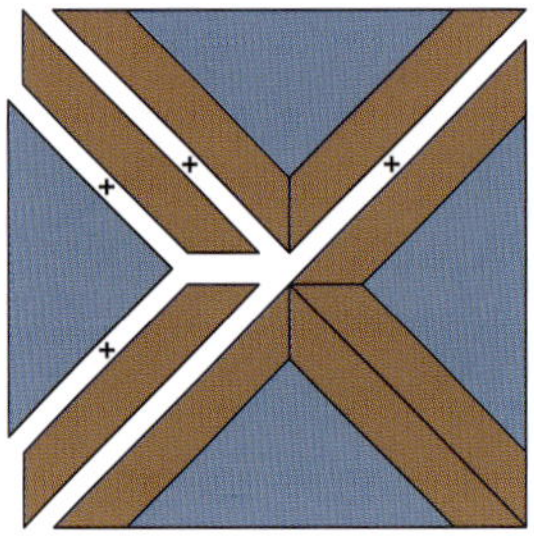

Construction

Sew the block, using the diagram as a guide. Assemble the triangular sections first, following the tips on inset seams (page 34).

56 Yosegi yabane

(Arrow feathers)

Woven stripes are often reversible, so you can use both sides of the fabric. To tessellate this block, reverse the position of light and dark patches.

CUTTING LIST

A

B

C

D

Cut 3⅛-in. (7.9-cm) wide strips of each fabric, with the stripes running parallel to the long edge. Cut these into the following pieces, using the 60-degree angle on your quilter's ruler (the measurements for each piece refer to the shorter cut edges).

A Eight 2 in. (5 cm) pieces.
B Eight 2 in. (5 cm) pieces.
C Four 2 in. (5 cm) pieces.
D Four 2 in. (5 cm) pieces.

Cut down the pieces for the top and bottom edges of the block so that the shortest vertical edge on the top pieces measures 1⅞ in. (4.8 cm) and on the bottom pieces measures 1 in. (2.5 cm).

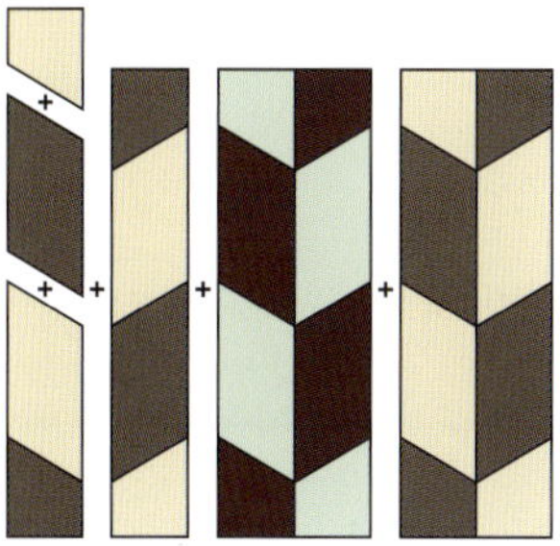

Construction

Sew the block, using the diagram as a guide. Take care not to stretch the bias edges as you sew. The block is assembled in strips.

57 Yosegi hoshi

(Star)

CUTTING LIST

A

B

C

Cut 2⅜-in. (6-cm) wide strips of A and B. Any stripes in the fabric should be parallel to the long edge of the strips. Cut star segments from these using the 45-degree angle on your quilter's ruler (the measurements for each piece refer to the shorter cut edges).

A Four 3⅛ in. (7.9 cm) pieces.
B Four 3⅛ in. (7.9 cm) pieces (mirror images of A pieces).
C Four 3¼ in. (8.3 cm) squares.
C One 4¾ in. (12 cm) square, cut in quarters diagonally.

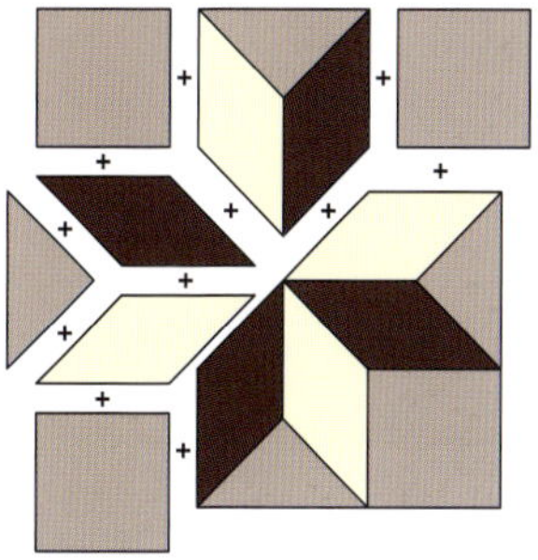

Construction

Sew the block, using the diagram as a guide. Assemble pairs of star segments first, then complete the block, following the tips on inset seams (page 34).

58 Kikkō

(Hexagons)

Woven stripes are often reversible, so you can use both sides of the fabric in order to have more flexibility matching the stripes. An ikat striped fabric gives a variety of colours. The finished block is 10¾ in. (27.3 cm) long, so trim it to a 9½ in. (24 cm) square if you wish, as shown here.

CUTTING LIST

A

Cut two strips of fabric, one 2¼ in. (5.7 cm) wide and the other 2¾ in. (7 cm) wide. Any stripes in the fabric should be parallel to the long edge of the strips. Cut triangles from these using the 60-degree angle on your quilter's ruler (the measurements for each piece refer to the equilateral cut edges). Use the photo to check the way the stripes run before cutting.

A Sixty-six 2 9/16 in. (6.5 cm) triangles from 2¼-in. (5.7-cm) wide strip.

A Six 3⅛ in. (7.9 cm) triangles from 2¾-in. (7-cm) wide strip, cut in half to produce right-angled triangles.

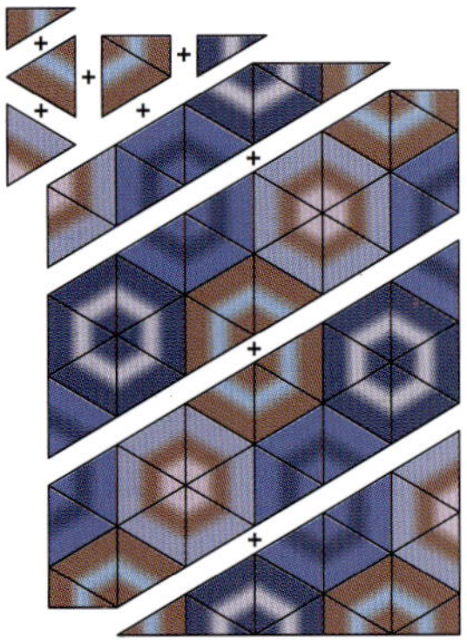

Construction

Sew the block, using the diagram as a guide. Arrange the triangles so that the stripes create a hexagon pattern. Take care not to stretch the bias edges as you sew. The block is assembled in rows.

59 Yosegi hishiseigaiha

(Diamond wave)

Use a fabric with shaded stripes to give the illusion of peaked waves. The finished block is 10¾ in. (27.3 cm) long, so trim it to a 9½ in. (24 cm) square if you wish, as shown here.

CUTTING LIST

A

Cut two strips of fabric, one 2¼ in. (5.7 cm) wide and the other 2¾ in. (7 cm) wide. Any stripes in the fabric should be parallel to the long edge of the strips. Cut triangles from these using the 60-degree angle on your quilter's ruler (the measurements for each piece refer to the equilateral cut edges). Use the photo to check the way the stripes run before cutting.

A Sixty-six 2 9/16 in. (6.5 cm) triangles from 2¼-in. (5.7-cm) wide strip.

A Six 3⅛ in. (7.9 cm) triangles from 2¾-in. (7-cm) wide strip, cut in half to produce right-angled triangles.

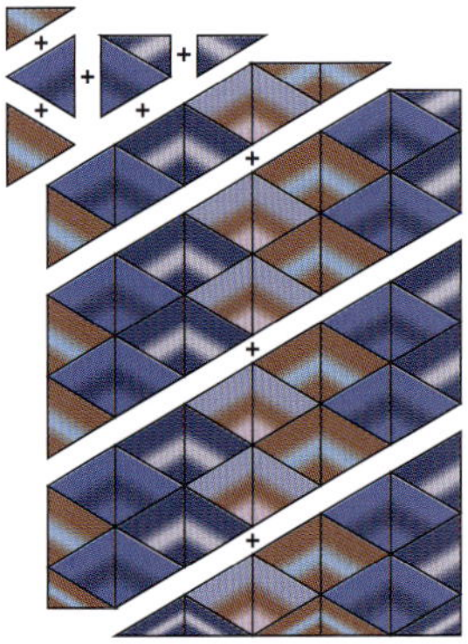

Construction

Sew the block, using the diagram as a guide. Arrange the triangles so that the stripes create a diamond wave pattern. Take care not to stretch the bias edges as you sew. The block is assembled in rows.

60 Yosegi uroko

(Scale variation)

Use the leftover triangles from blocks 58 and 59 to make this design. The finished block is 10¾ in. (27.3 cm) long, so trim it to a 9½ in. (24 cm) square if you wish, as shown here.

CUTTING LIST

A 

B 

Cut 2¼-in. (5.7-cm) and 2¾-in. (7-cm) wide strips of A and B. Any stripes in the fabric should be parallel to the long edge of the strips. Cut triangles from these using the 60-degree angle on your quilter's ruler (the measurements for each piece refer to the equilateral cut edges). Use the photo to check the way the stripes run before cutting.

- A Thirty-three 2$\frac{9}{16}$ in. (6.5 cm) triangles from 2¼-in. (5.7-cm) wide strip.
- A Three 3⅛ in. (7.9 cm) triangles from 2¾-in. (7-cm) wide strip, cut in half to produce right-angled triangles.
- B Thirty-three 2$\frac{9}{16}$ in. (6.5 cm) triangles from 2¼-in. (5.7-cm) wide strip.
- B Three 3⅛ in. (7.9 cm) triangles from 2¾-in. (7-cm) wide strip, cut in half to produce right-angled triangles.

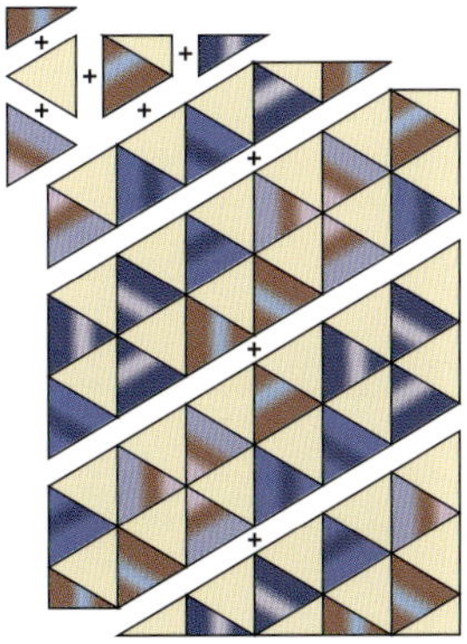

Construction

Sew the block, using the diagram as a guide. Arrange the striped triangles so that the top points of groups of three triangles meet together. Take care not to stretch the bias edges as you sew. The block is assembled in rows.

Mix & Match

ideas for combining blocks

Above, from top left: 8 x block 58 (untrimmed); 1 each x blocks 106, 103, 104 and 109; 4 x block 59 (untrimmed). Below, from top left: 21 x block 36; 21 x block 39.

61 Yosegi matsukawabishi

(Pine bark diamond)

To tessellate the pattern, make a mirror image of the design and place the two blocks side by side. The finished block is 10¾ in. (27.3 cm) long, so trim it to a 9½ in. (24 cm) square if you wish, as shown here.

CUTTING LIST

A

B

Cut 2¼-in. (5.7-cm), 2-in. (5-cm), and 1½-in. (3.8-cm) wide strips of A. Cut a 1-in. (2.5-cm) wide strip of B. Cut the pieces from these using the 60-degree angle on your quilter's ruler (the measurements for each piece refer to the cut edges).

- A Twelve $2\frac{9}{16}$ in. (6.5 cm) triangles from wide strip.
- A Fifteen $2\frac{9}{16}$ in. (7.9 cm) diamonds from medium strip; cut three of them in half lengthways.
- A Fifteen 1¾ in. (4.4 cm) diamonds from narrow strip.
- B Eighteen 2¼-in. (5.7-cm) long parallelograms with slant to left and three with slant to right.
- B Fifteen 1¾-in. (4.4-cm) long parallelograms with slant to right.

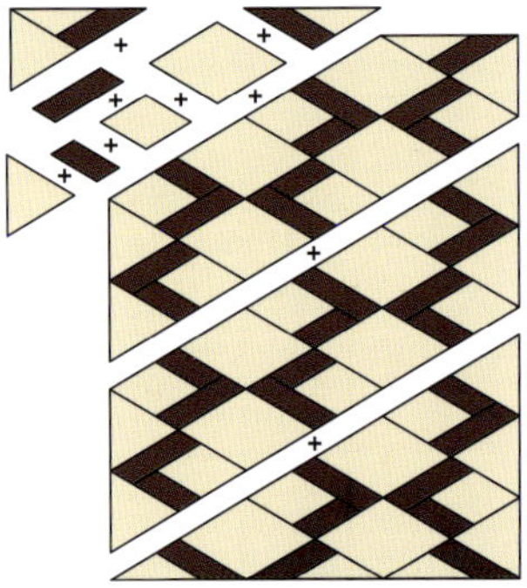

Construction

Sew the block, using the diagram as a guide. Use the half-diamonds for the top and bottom edges. Take care not to stretch the bias edges as you sew. The block is assembled in rows. When the block is complete, trim the top and bottom straight.

62 Pieced kagome

(Bamboo basket)

To tessellate the pattern horizontally, make alternate blocks with the central strip of hexagons used on the outside, and the outer strip in the centre. The finished block is 10¾ in. (27.3 cm) long, so trim it to a 9½ in. (24 cm) square if you wish, as shown here.

CUTTING LIST

A B C D E F

- A Sixteen triangles with $2\frac{9}{16}$ in. (6.5 cm) equilateral sides cut from a 2¼-in. (5.7-cm) wide strip of fabric using the 60-degree angle on your quilter's ruler.
- A Two $1\frac{11}{16}$ x 3 in. (4.3 x 7.6 cm) strips, cut in half diagonally with one slanting up to the right and the other down to the right.
- B Four 2 in. (5 cm) half-hexagons.
- C Two 2 in. (5 cm) hexagons.
- D Two 2 in. (5 cm) hexagons.
- E Two 2 in. (5 cm) hexagons.
- F One 2 in. (5 cm) hexagon.

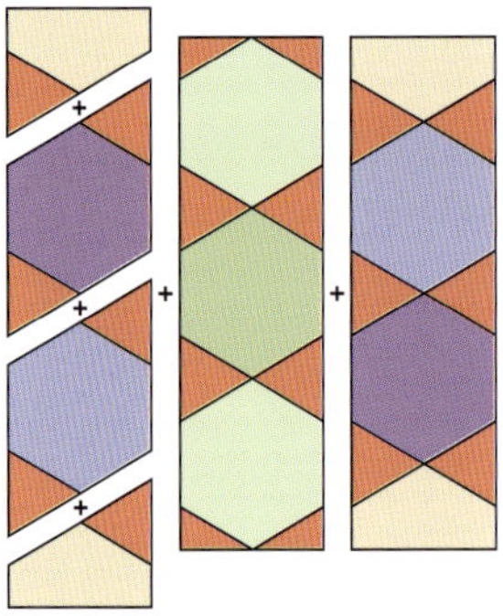

Construction

Sew the block, using the diagram as a guide. Take care not to stretch the bias edges as you sew. The block is assembled in columns.

63 Kasane kikkō variation

(Layered tortoiseshell variation)

Use a different fabric for the central hexagon if you prefer. Choose one that tones well with the outer hexagons. The finished block is $10\frac{3}{4}$ in. (27.3 cm) long, so trim it to a $9\frac{1}{2}$ in. (24 cm) square if you wish, as shown here.

CUTTING LIST

A 

B 

C 

D 

E 

A Eighteen $1\frac{11}{16}$ x 3 in. (4.3 x 7.6 cm) strips, cut in half diagonally with nine slanting up to the right and nine down to the right.
B Three 2 in. (5 cm) hexagons.
C Two 2 in. (5 cm) hexagons.
D Two 2 in. (5 cm) hexagons.
E Two 2 in. (5 cm) hexagons.

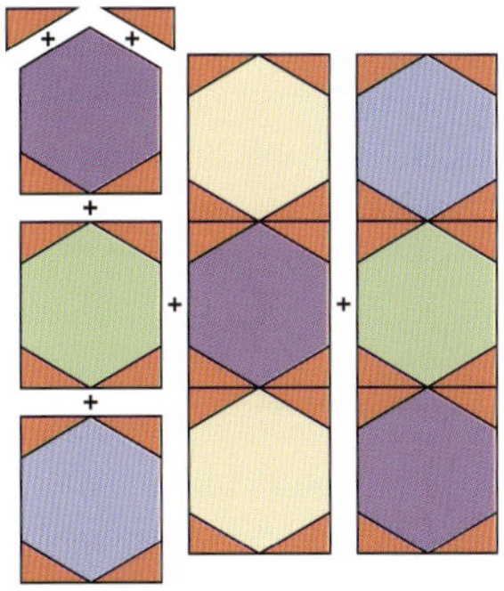

Construction

Sew the block, using the diagram as a guide. Take care not to stretch the bias edges as you sew. The block is assembled in columns.

64 Yosegi kikkō variation

(Tortoiseshell variation)

Cut the pieced hexagons from a fabric with wide stripes to create a simpler version of this block. The finished block is $10\frac{3}{4}$ in. (27.3 cm) long, so trim it to a $9\frac{1}{2}$ in. (24 cm) square if you wish, as shown here.

CUTTING LIST

A 

B 

A Several 2-in. (5-cm) wide strips.
A Several $1\frac{1}{4}$-in. (3.2-cm) wide strips.
B Several $1\frac{1}{4}$-in. (3.2-cm) wide strips.

Whole hexagons: Sew a B strip to each side of a wide A strip, then cut eight 2 in. (5 cm) hexagons from these.
Part-hexagons at top and bottom: Sew a wide A strip and B strip together, then cut four 2 in. (5 cm) part-hexagons from these.
Part-hexagons at sides and corners: Sew a narrow A strip and B strip together, then cut six 2 in. (5 cm) part-hexagons from these.
Refer to page 33 for tips on this quick piecing method.

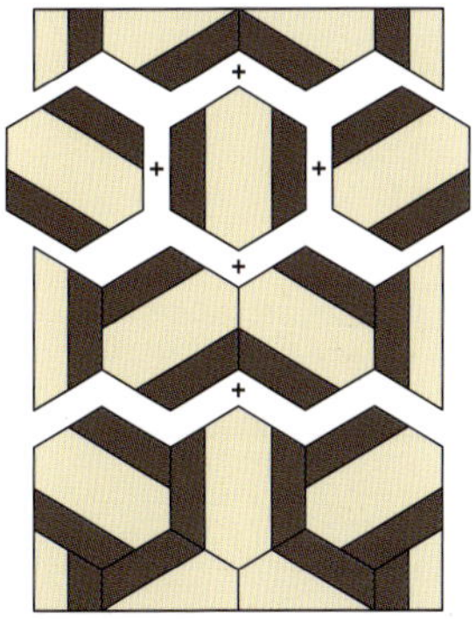

Construction

Sew the block, using the diagram as a guide. The block is assembled in strips. Complete the block, following the tips on inset seams (page 34), then trim the top and bottom straight.

65 Kasane kikkō

(Layered tortoiseshell)

The finished block is $10\frac{3}{4}$ in. (27.3 cm) long, so trim it to a $9\frac{1}{2}$ in. (24 cm) square if you wish, as shown here.

CUTTING LIST

A B C D E

Cut 2-in. (5-cm) and $2\frac{1}{4}$-in. (5.7-cm) wide strips of A. Cut the diamonds and equilateral triangles from these using the 60-degree angle on your quilter's ruler (the measurements for each piece refer to the cut edges).

- A Eight $2\frac{1}{4}$ in. (5.7 cm) diamonds from narrow strip.
- A Four $2\frac{9}{16}$ in. (6.5 cm) equilateral triangles from wide strip.
- A Two $1\frac{11}{16}$ x 3 in. (4.3 x 7.6 cm) strips, cut in half diagonally with one slanting up to the right and the other down to the right.
- B Three 2 in. (5 cm) hexagons.
- C Two 2 in. (5 cm) hexagons.
- D Two 2 in. (5 cm) hexagons.
- E Two 2 in. (5 cm) hexagons.

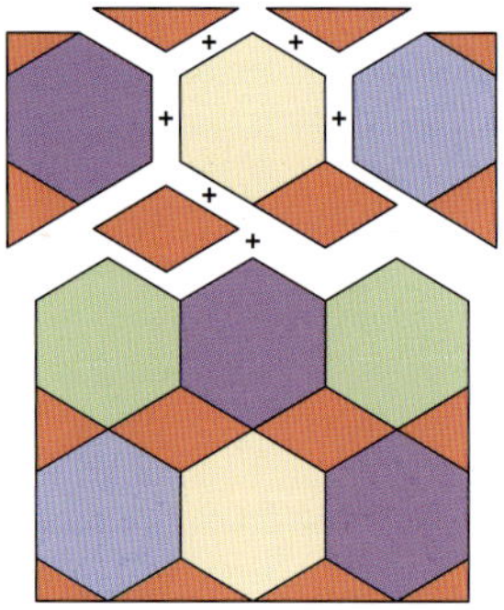

Construction

Sew the block, using the diagram as a guide. Complete the block, following the tips on inset seams (page 34), then trim the top and bottom straight.

66 Bishamon kikkō variation

(Bishamon tortoiseshell)

The finished block is $10\frac{3}{4}$ in. (27.3 cm) long, so trim it to a $9\frac{1}{2}$ in. (24 cm) square if you wish, as shown here.

CUTTING LIST

A B C

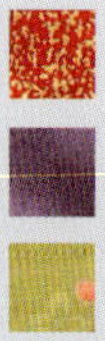

- A Two $1\frac{11}{16}$ x 3 in. (4.3 x 7.6 cm) strips.
- A Eight 2 in. (5 cm) half-hexagons.
- B One $1\frac{11}{16}$ x 3 in. (4.3 x 7.6 cm) strip.
- B Nine 2 in. (5 cm) half-hexagons.
- C One $1\frac{11}{16}$ x 3 in. (4.3 x 7.6 cm) strip.
- C Nine 2 in. (5 cm) half-hexagons.

Cut all the strips in half diagonally, with an A and C strip slanting up to the right and the other A and B strip down to the right.

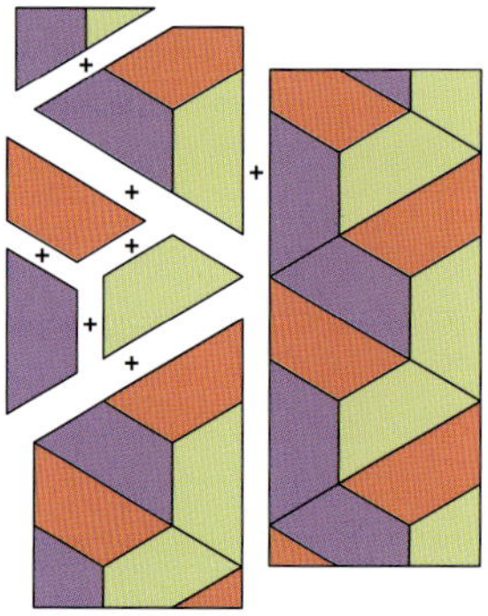

Construction

Sew the block, using the diagram as a guide. Complete the block, following the tips on inset seams (page 34), then trim the top and bottom straight. Use the spare small B and C triangles for another block.

67 Mukai kikkō yamagata variation

(Facing tortoiseshell mountain form)

The finished block is 10¾ in. (27.3 cm) long, so trim it to a 9½ in. (24 cm) square if you wish, as shown here.

CUTTING LIST

A, B, C, D

Cut 2-in. (5-cm) wide strips of B and C and a 2¼-in. (5.7-cm) wide strip of D. Cut the diamonds and equilateral triangles from these using the 60-degree angle on your quilter's ruler (the measurements for each piece refer to the cut edges).

- A Two 1 11/16 x 3 in. (4.3 x 7.6 cm) strips. Also cut one in B and one in C.
- A Eight 2 in. (5 cm) half-hexagons. Also cut five in B, five in C and four in D.
- B One 2¼ in. (5.7 cm) diamond.
- C One 2¼ in. (5.7 cm) diamond.
- D Four 2 9/16 in. (6.5 cm) equilateral triangles.

Cut the strips in half diagonally, with an A and B strip slanting up to the right and an A and C strip down to the right.

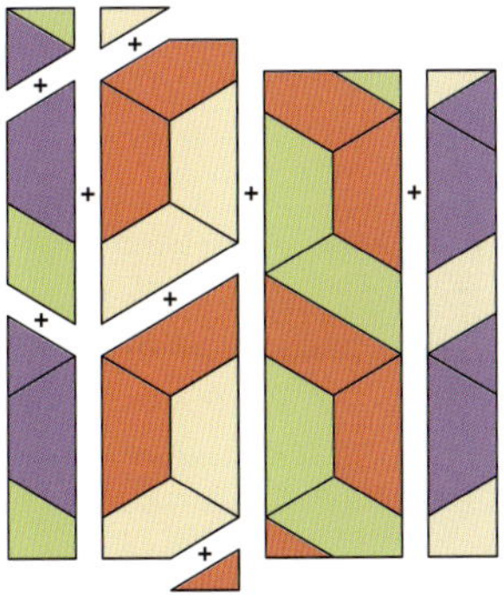

Construction

Sew the block, using the diagram as a guide. Complete the block, following the tips on inset seams (page 34), then trim the top and bottom straight. Use the spare small A triangles for another block.

68 Kimono

CUTTING LIST

A, B

- A Two 9 x 2¾ in. (22.9 x 7 cm) strips.
- A Two 3½ x 2¾ in. (8.9 x 7 cm) strips.
- A One 2¼ x 1 in. (5.7 x 2.5 cm) strip.
- B Two 6 x 2¾ in. (15.2 x 7 cm) strips.
- B Two 4⅝ x 1 in. (11.7 x 2.5 cm) strips.

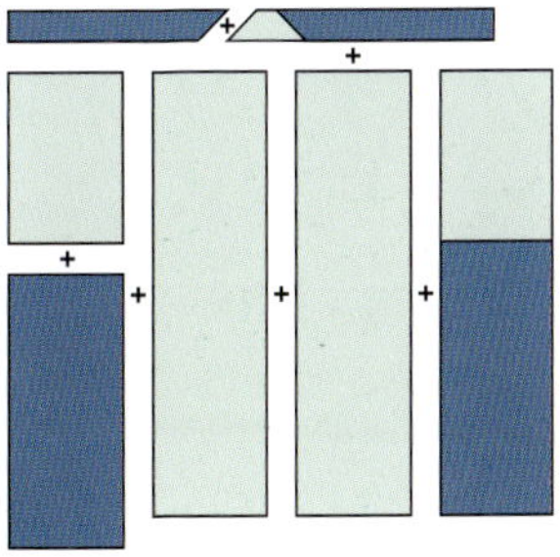

Construction

Sew the block, using the diagram as a guide. The block is assembled in strips. Sew the collar piece to the narrow strips with 45-degree seams using the sewing mitres method (page 35).

69 Komon kimono (Small pattern)

You will have twice as many side skirt triangles as you need, so cut additional strips to sew a second block if you wish. For reversible fabrics, use the instructions for block 70.

CUTTING LIST

A 

B 

- A Two 9 x 2¾ in. (22.9 x 7 cm) strips.
- A Two 3½ x 2¾ in. (8.9 x 7 cm) strips.
- A One 2¼ x 1 in. (5.7 x 2.5 cm) strip.
- A Two 5½ x 3¾ in. (14 x 9.5 cm) strips, placed right sides together and cut in half diagonally.
- B Two 5¼ x 2⅞ in. (13.3 x 7.3 cm) strips, placed right sides together and cut in half diagonally.
- B Two 2⅛ x 3¼ in. (5.4 x 8.3 cm) strips, placed right sides together and cut in half diagonally.
- B Two 4⅝ x 1 in. (11.7 x 2.5 cm) strips.

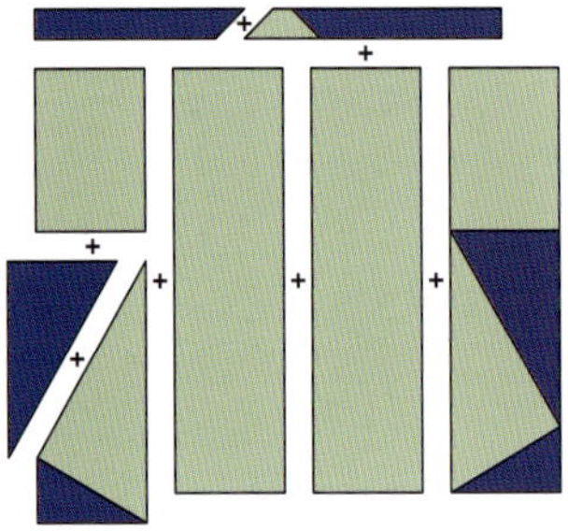

Construction

Sew the block, using the diagram as a guide. Make the side skirts first, taking care not to stretch the bias edges as you sew. Assemble the block in strips in the same way as block 68.

70 Striped kimono

This block is suitable for reversible fabrics only. Stripes can be horizontal or vertical. For non-reversible fabrics, use the instructions for block 69.

CUTTING LIST

A 

B 

- A Two 9 x 2¾ in. (22.9 x 7 cm) strips.
- A Two 3½ x 2¾ in. (8.9 x 7 cm) strips.
- A One 2¼ x 1 in. (5.7 x 2.5 cm) strip.
- A One 5½ x 3¾ in. (14 x 9.5 cm) strip, cut in half diagonally.
- B One 5¼ x 2⅞ in. (13.3 x 7.3 cm) strip, cut in half diagonally.
- B One 2⅛ x 3¼ in. (5.4 x 8.3 cm) strip, cut in half diagonally.
- B Two 4⅝ x 1 in. (11.7 x 2.5 cm) strips.

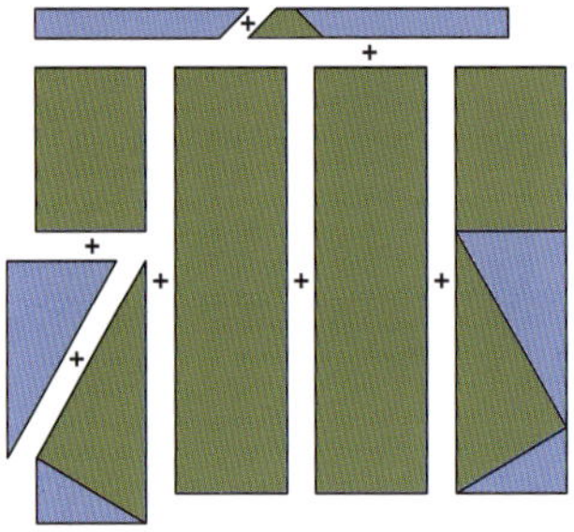

Construction

Sew the block, using the diagram as a guide. Make one side skirt using the front of the triangles; make the second skirt using the reverse. Take care not to stretch the bias edges as you sew. Assemble the block in strips in the same way as block 68.

71 Somoyo kimono

(All-over pattern)

Kimono with large all-over patterns became popular in the 17th century. Cut the kimono pieces so that the pattern flows over the back and sleeves. Use a reversible plain fabric for the background.

CUTTING LIST

A 

B 

- A One 9 x 5 in. (22.9 x 12.7 cm) strip.
- A Two 3½ x 2¾ in. (8.9 x 7 cm) strips.
- A One 2¼ x 1 in. (5.7 x 2.5 cm) strip.
- A Two 5½ x 3¾ in. (14 x 9.5 cm) strips, placed right sides together and cut in half diagonally.
- B One 5¼ x 2⅞ in. (13.3 x 7.3 cm) strips, cut in half diagonally.
- B One 2⅛ x 3¼ in. (5.4 x 8.3 cm) strips, cut in half diagonally.
- B Two 4⅝ x 1 in. (11.7 x 2.5 cm) strips.

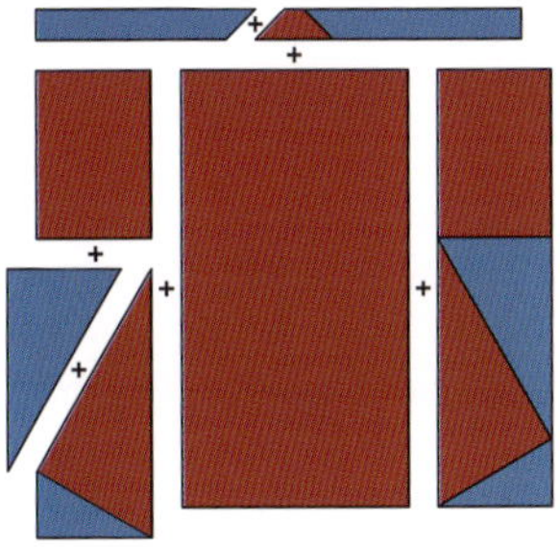

Construction

Sew the block, using the diagram as a guide. Make the side skirts first, using the front and reverse of the B triangles (as block 70). Two A skirt triangles will be left over. Take care not to stretch the bias edges as you sew. Assemble the block in strips in the same way as block 68.

Mix & Match

ideas for combining blocks

Above, from top left: 1 each x kamon blocks 114, 116 and 115; 1 each x kimono blocks 70, 71, 68, 73, 72 and 69; 6 x patchwork block 50.

72 Furisode kimono

(Flutter sleeve)

Large patterns are often used for furisode, worn by unmarried girls. Cut the kimono pieces so that the pattern flows over the back and sleeves. Use a reversible fabric for the background.

CUTTING LIST

A
B

- A One 9 x 5 in. (22.9 x 12.7 cm) strip.
- A Two 6 x 2¾ in. (15.2 x 7 cm) strips.
- A One 2¼ x 1 in. (5.7 x 2.5 cm) strip.
- A Two 5½ x 3¾ in. (14 x 9.5 cm) strips, cut in half diagonally.
- B One 2⅛ x 3¼ in. (5.4 x 8.3 cm) strip, cut in half diagonally.
- B One 5¼ x 2⅞ in. (13.3 x 7.3 cm) strip, cut in half diagonally.
- B Two 4⅝ x 1 in. (11.7 x 2.5 cm) strips.

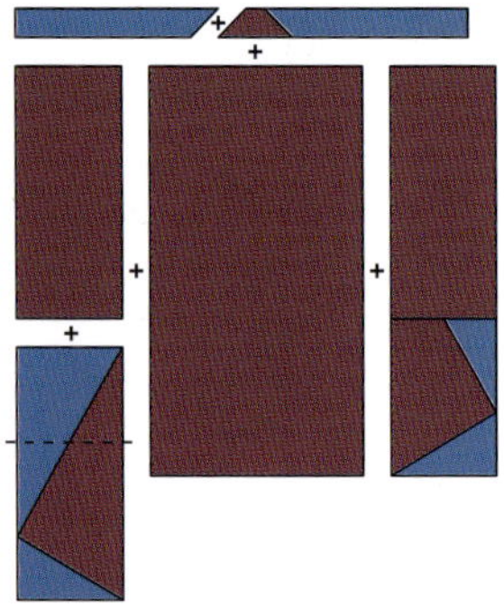

Construction

Sew the block, using the diagram as a guide. Make the side skirts first (as block 71). Trim the skirts to 4 in. (10 cm) long, as indicated by the dashed line, and discard the upper sections. Assemble the block in strips in the same way as block 68.

73 Patchwork kimono

Patchwork kimono were worn as under-kimono in a two-layered kasane set. They are worn today as dance costumes at the Nishimonai summer festival. Use reversible fabrics for A and F, or cut the skirt pieces as for block 69.

CUTTING LIST

A
B
C
D
E
F

- A Two 2½ x 1 in. (6.4 x 2.5 cm) strips.
- A Two 2½ x 2¾ in. (6.4 x 7 cm) strips.
- A One 5½ x 3¾ in. (14 x 9.5 cm) strip, cut in half diagonally.
- B Two 6 x 1 in. (15.2 x 2.5 cm) strips. Repeat in D and E.
- B Two 1½ x 2¾ in. (3.8 x 7 cm) strips.
- C Two 1½ x 1 in. (3.8 x 2.5 cm) strips.
- C Two 3½ x 1 in. (8.9 x 2.5 cm) strips.
- C Two 6 x 1¼ in. (15.2 x 3.2 cm) strips.
- D One 2¼ x 1 in. (5.7 x 2.5 cm) strip.
- E Two 3½ x 1¾ in. (8.9 x 4.4 cm) strips.
- F One 2⅛ x 3¼ in. (5.4 x 8.3 cm) strip, cut in half diagonally.
- F One 5¼ x 2⅞ in. (13.3 x 7.3 cm) strip, cut in half diagonally.
- F Two 4⅝ x 1 in. (11.7 x 2.5 cm) strips.

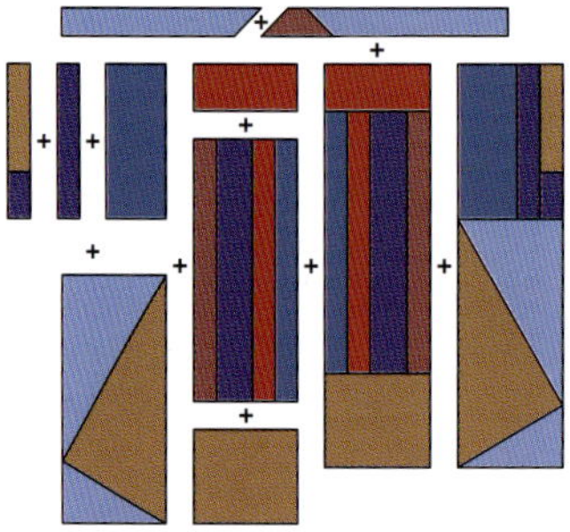

Construction

Sew the block, using the diagram as a guide. Make one side skirt using the front of the triangles; make the second skirt using the reverse. Take care not to stretch the bias edges as you sew. Assemble the block in strips in the same way as block 68.

74 Fujisan

(Mount Fuji)

The triangle point of the central strip will be 'cut off' slightly when sewn to the strip above, making Mount Fuji the right shape.

CUTTING LIST

A One 5 x 9½ in. (12.7 x 24 cm) strip.
B One 3 x 9½ in. (7.6 x 24 cm) strip.
C Two 3 x 5¾ in. (7.6 x 14.6 cm) strips, placed right sides together and cut in half diagonally.
C One 2½ x 9½ in. (6.4 x 24 cm) strip.

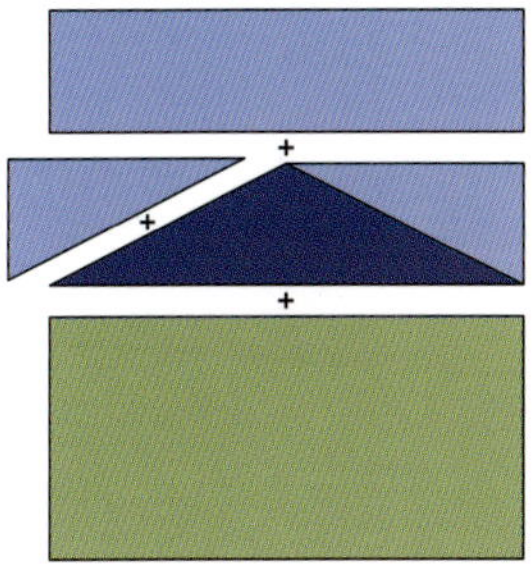

Construction

Sew the block, using the diagram as a guide. Start by sewing the C triangles to the B strip (page 37), then sew the remaining pieces together. Two C triangles will be left over, so use these for another block.

75 Torii

(Sacred gate)

Fusible bias tape makes the curved top of the gate easy to shape.

CUTTING LIST

A One 2½ x 9½ in. (6.4 x 24 cm) strip.
B One 3 x 9½ in. (7.6 x 24 cm) strip.
C Two 3 x 5¾ in. (7.6 x 14.6 cm) strips, placed right sides together and cut in half diagonally.
C One 3½ x 9½ in. (8.9 x 24 cm) strip.
C One 2½ x 9½ in. (6.4 x 24 cm) strip.
D Two 1 x 8¾ in. (2.5 x 22.2 cm) strips.
D One 1¼ x 7¼ in. (3.2 x 18.4 cm) strip.
D About 2 ft. (60 cm) of ¼-in. (6-mm) wide fusible bias tape.

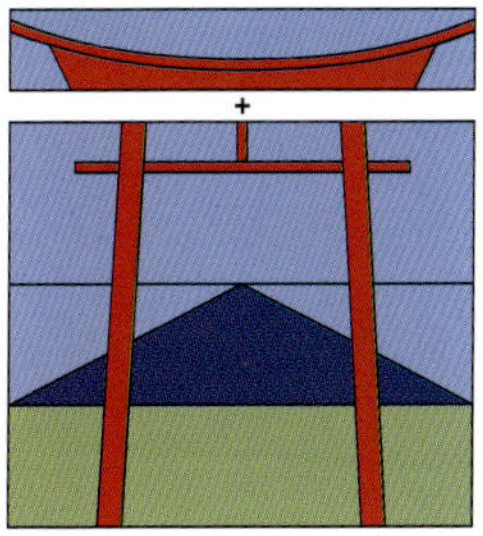

Construction

Sew the block, using the diagram as a guide. Follow the assembly method on page 37, using the wide C strip for the sky above Mount Fuji and the narrow C strip for the top section. Use the narrow D strips for the sides of the gate and the wide strip for the top of the gate. Two C triangles will be left over, so use these for another block.

76 Minka

(Farmhouse)

Change the season in the landscape with your selection of fabrics.

CUTTING LIST

- A One 1½ x 9½ in. (3.8 x 24 cm) strip.
- A Two 1¼ x 2½ in. (3.2 x 6.4 cm) strips.
- A Two 2½ in. (6.4 cm) squares.
- B One 2 x 8 in. (5 x 20.3 cm) strip.
- C One 2½ x 9½ in. (6.4 x 24 cm) strip.
- D One 1¼ x 5½ in. (3.2 x 14 cm) strip.
- E One 2 x 9½ in. (5 x 24 cm) strip.
- F One 4 in. (10.2 cm) square, cut in half diagonally.
- F One 2½ in. (6.4 cm) square, cut in half diagonally.
- F One 2⅛ in. (5.4 cm) square.
- G One 3½ in. (8.9 cm) square, cut in quarters diagonally.
- H Two 1¼ x 2 in. (3.2 x 5 cm) strips.

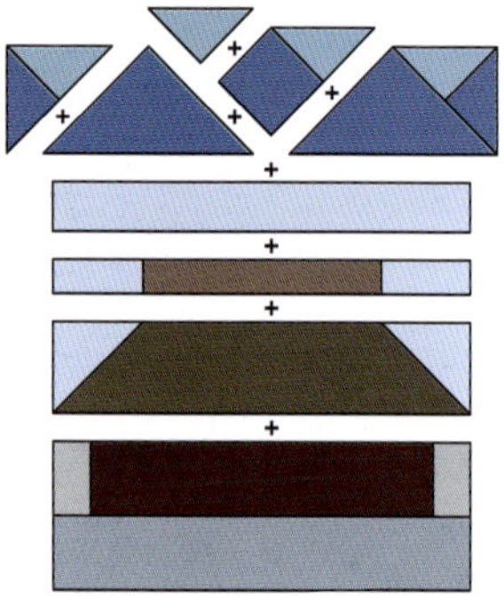

Construction

Sew the block, using the diagram as a guide. Sew the A squares onto each end of the C strip using the fast corners method (page 37) to form the roof of the house. The block is assembled in strips.

77 Mura

(Village)

Select fabrics resembling thatch, wood and so on to add realism to the houses.

CUTTING LIST

- A One 4⅜ in. (11.1 cm) square, cut in half diagonally.
- A Two 1¼ x 2 in. (3.2 x 5 cm) strips.
- A One 2⅞ in. (7.3 cm) square, cut in half diagonally.
- A Two 1 x 1½ in. (2.5 x 3.8 cm) strips.
- B One 3½ x 5½ in. (8.9 x 14 cm) strip.
- C One 2 x 6 in. (5 x 15.2 cm) strip.
- C One 1½ x 3½ in. (3.8 x 8.9 cm) strip.
- D One right-angled triangle, 2⅞ in. (7.3 cm) high at centre and 5¾ in. (13.3 cm) wide at base.
- D One right-angled triangle, 4⅛ in. (10.5 cm) high at centre and 8¼ in. (21 cm) wide at base.
- E One 6½ x 2½ in. (16.5 x 6.4 cm) strip.
- F One 1½ x 7½ in. (3.8 x 19 cm) strip.

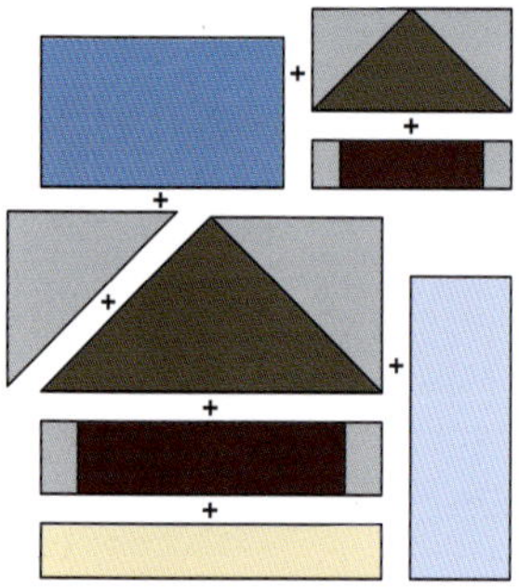

Construction

Sew the block, using the diagram as a guide. Assemble the two houses first, taking care not to stretch the bias edges as you sew, then complete the block.

78 Pieced ōgi

(Folding fan)

A large-scale print looks very effective for the fan.

CUTTING LIST

A One 9½ in. (24 cm) square.
B Four fan paper pieces using template enlarged by 400%.

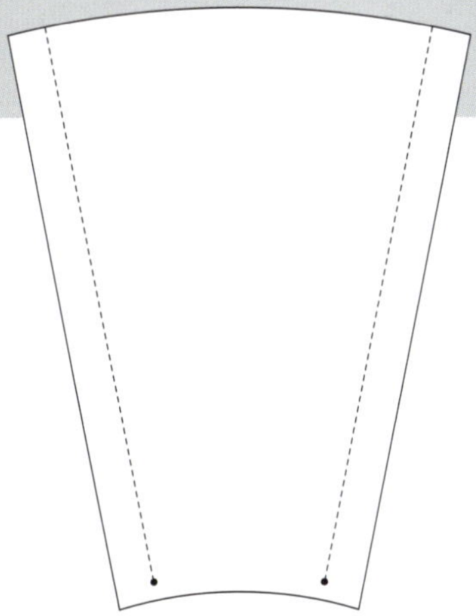

Construction

Sew the block, using the diagram as a guide. Sew the four fan paper pieces together, finishing each seam at the dot, then press the seams open. Appliqué the completed fan paper to the background square. Refer to pages 38–39 for tips on appliqué.

79 Kiku

(Chrysanthemum)

CUTTING LIST

A One 9½ in. (24 cm) square.
B Eight petals using template enlarged by 250%.
C One 2-in. (5-cm) diameter circle.

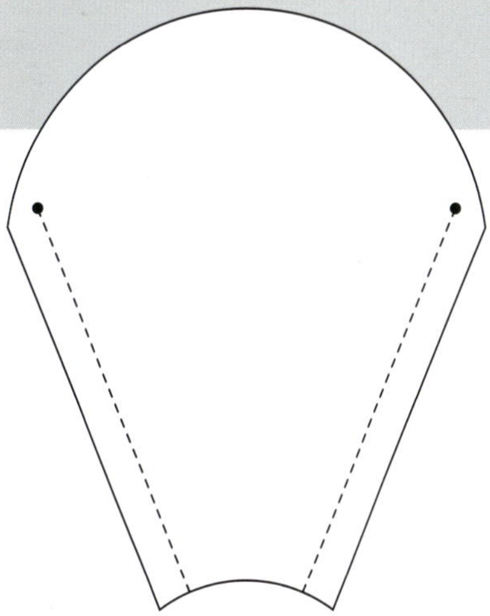

Construction

Sew the block, using the diagram as a guide. Sew the eight petals together, finishing each seam at the dot, then press the seams open. Appliqué the petals to the background square, then appliqué the circle in place to cover the raw edges. Refer to pages 38–39 for tips on appliqué.

80 Meisen momiji kōshi

(Meisen silk maple check)

Choose a C fabric with a well-defined motif that you can cut out and appliqué easily.

CUTTING LIST

A
B
C

A One 5½ x 4½ in. (14 x 11.4 cm) strip.
A One 1 x 4½ in. (2.5 x 11.4 cm) strip.
A Two 1 x 4 in. (2.5 x 10.2 cm) strips.
B One 3 x 1½ in. (7.6 x 3.8 cm) strip.
B One 3 x 5½ in. (7.6 x 14 cm) strip.
C One 4 x 3½ in. (10.2 x 8.9 cm) strip.
C One 6 x 5½ in. (15.2 x 14 cm) strip.
C Motifs for appliqué.

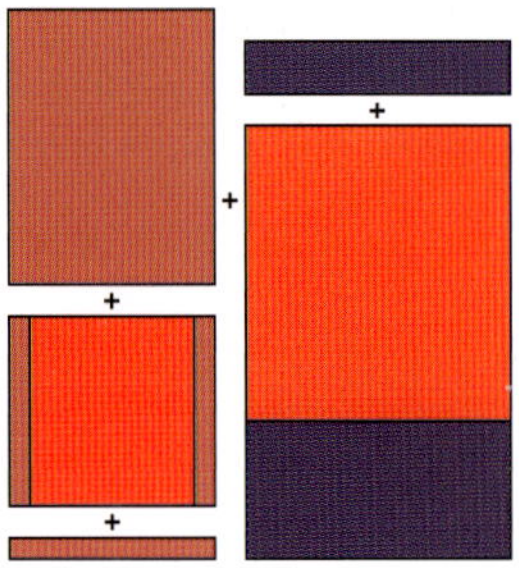

Construction

Sew the block, using the diagram as a guide. The block is assembled in strips. Appliqué the motifs last. Refer to pages 38–39 for tips on appliqué.

81 Meisen momiji kōshi no.2

(Meisen silk maple check no.2)

Choose a C fabric with a well-defined motif that you can cut out and appliqué easily.

CUTTING LIST

A
B
C
D
E

A One 2½ x 9 in. (6.4cm x 22.9 cm) strip.
A Two 2½ x 5½ in. (6.4 x 14 cm) strips.
A One 3 x 1 in. (7.6 x 2.5 cm) strip.
B One 9½ x 2½ in. (24 x 6.4 cm) strip.
C Two 3 in. (7.6 cm) squares.
C Motifs for appliqué.
D Two 2½ x 3 in. (6.4 x 7.6 cm) strips.
E Two 1 x 2½ in. (2.5 x 6.4 cm) strips.
E One 1 x 5 in. (2.5 x 12.7 cm) strip.

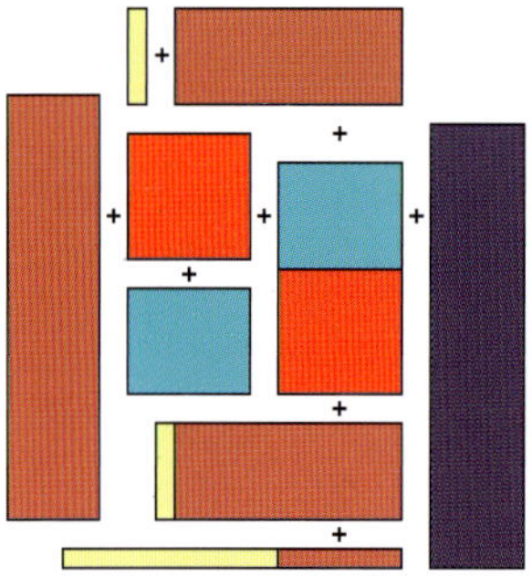

Construction

Sew the block, using the diagram as a guide. Appliqué the motifs last. Refer to pages 38–39 for tips on appliqué.

82 Boromono

(Rag block)

This is an ideal block for using up scraps of fabric. Vary the width and number of the strips as well as the size of the appliquéd circles, according to the scraps you have.

CUTTING LIST

A Six 9½ x 2 in. (24 x 5 cm) strips pieced from scraps of fabric.
B Two 3-in. (7.6-cm) diameter circles.
C One 3-in. (7.6-cm) diameter circle.

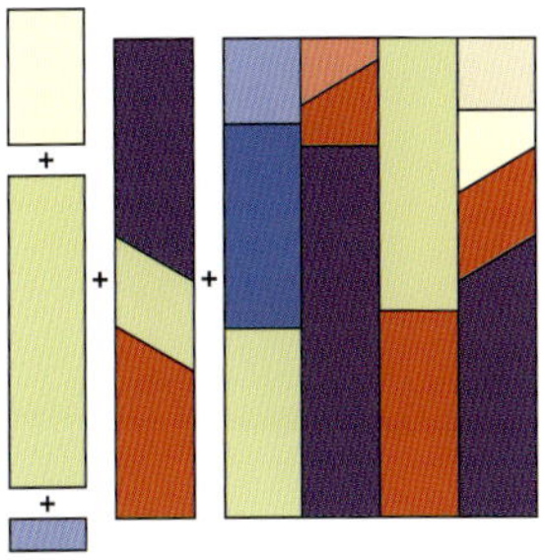

Construction

Sew the block, using the diagram as a guide. The block is assembled in strips and appliquéd with the circles last. Refer to pages 38–39 for tips on appliqué.

Mix & Match

ideas for combining blocks

Above, from top left: 21 x block 81 (blocks in 1st, 3rd and 5th rows are offset, with half-blocks at each end); 4 x block 46. Below, from top left: 20 x block 82 (alternate blocks are rotated 90 degrees); 1 each x blocks 119, 117, 118, 124 and 120.

83 Shippō

(Seven treasures)

The name is probably a pun on shi ho (four directions).

Stitching the sashiko

Cut out a 9½ in. (24 cm) square of fabric and mark a ¼ in. (6 mm) seam allowance all around it. Mark a 1½ in. (3.8 cm) base grid onto the central square. Use a 3-in. (7.6-cm) diameter circle template to mark the sashiko design. Following the red arrows on the diagram, stitch diagonal wavy lines. Stitch around the pattern in continuous lines. Refer to pages 40–41 for tips on sashiko stitching.

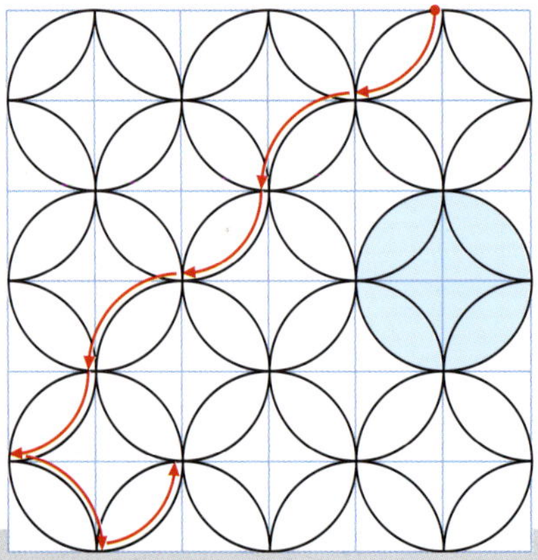

84 Fundō

(Balance weights)

Gold ingots were traditionally cast in this symmetrical shape.

Stitching the sashiko

Cut out a 9½ in. (24 cm) square of fabric and mark a ¼ in. (6 mm) seam allowance all around it. Mark a 1½ in. (3.8 cm) base grid onto the central square. Use a 3-in. (7.6-cm) diameter circle template to mark the sashiko design. Following the red and blue arrows on the diagram, stitch diagonal wavy lines. Stitch around the pattern in continuous lines. Refer to pages 40–41 for tips on sashiko stitching.

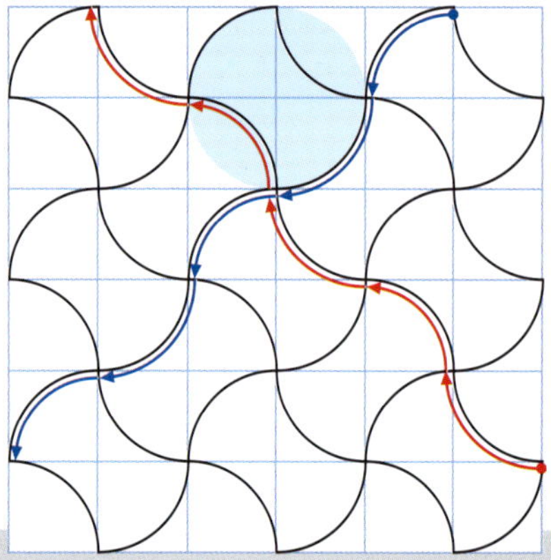

85 Raimon

(Spiral)

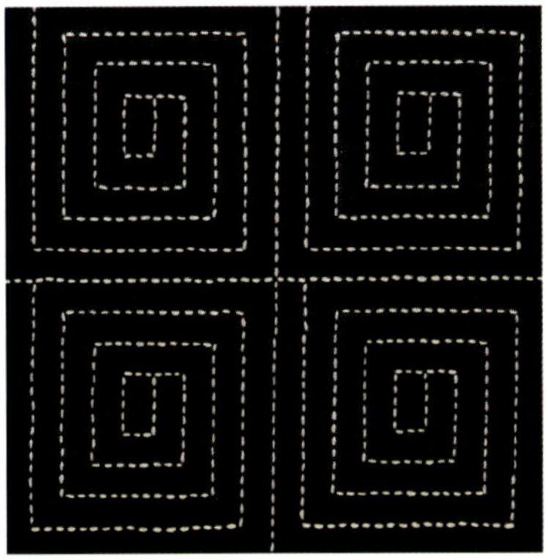

This is one of the oldest sashiko designs.

Stitching the sashiko

Cut out a 9½ in. (24 cm) square of fabric and mark a ¼ in. (6 mm) seam allowance all around it. Mark a 4½ in. (11.4 cm) base grid onto the central square, then mark spirals onto each of the four sections with lines at ½ in. (1.2 cm) intervals. Note that the diagram below shows only one spiral. Stitch vertical and horizontal lines through the centre of the grid. Following the red arrow on the diagram, stitch each spiral. Refer to pages 40–41 for tips on sashiko stitching.

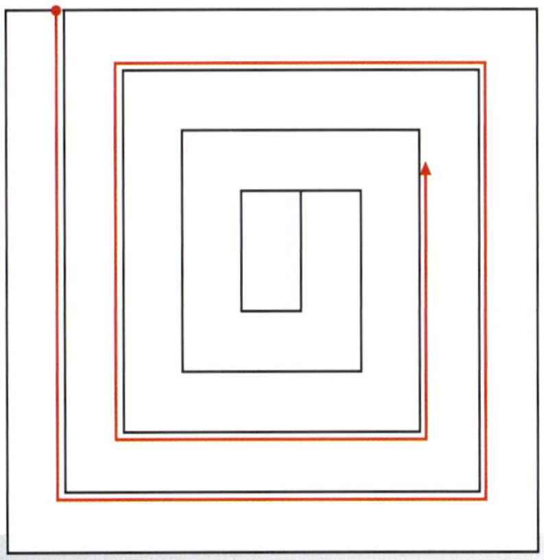

Mix & Match

ideas for combining blocks

Above, from centre out: 5 x block 44; 4 x block 45; 16 x block 83; 24 x block 10. Below, from top left: 10 x block 86; 15 x block 85.

86 Masuzashi

(Square measure sashiko)

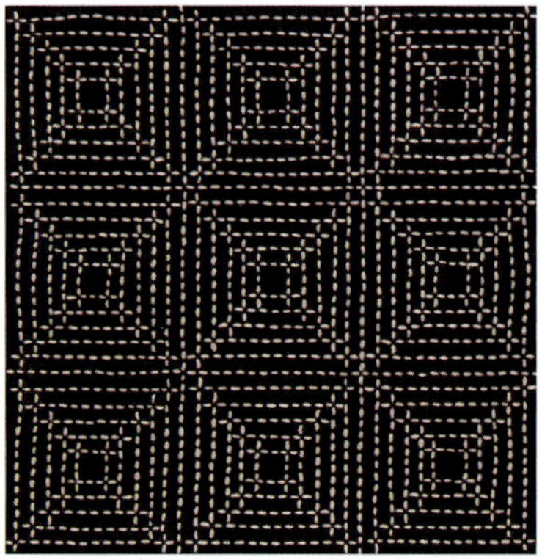

Masu are nesting wooden measuring boxes, used for dry goods and as sake cups.

Stitching the sashiko

Cut out a 9½ in. (24 cm) square of fabric and mark a ¼ in. (6 mm) seam allowance all around it. Mark a 3 in. (7.6 cm) base grid onto the central square. Using the diagram as a guide, mark nesting squares within each section of the grid with lines at ¼ in. (6 mm) intervals, crossing the lines at the corners. Note that the diagram below shows only one square. Stitch each nest of squares, starting with the largest square and spiraling inwards. Cross the stitching lines (but not the stitches) at each corner and strand across the back from one line to another. Refer to pages 40–41 for tips on sashiko stitching.

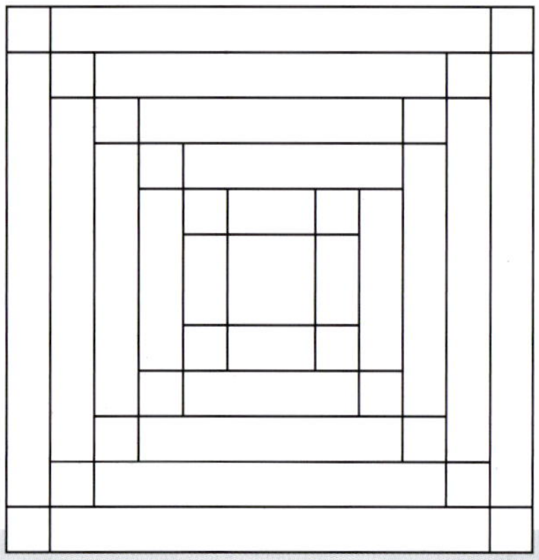

87 Hirai jūmon

(Crossed well curb or crosses)

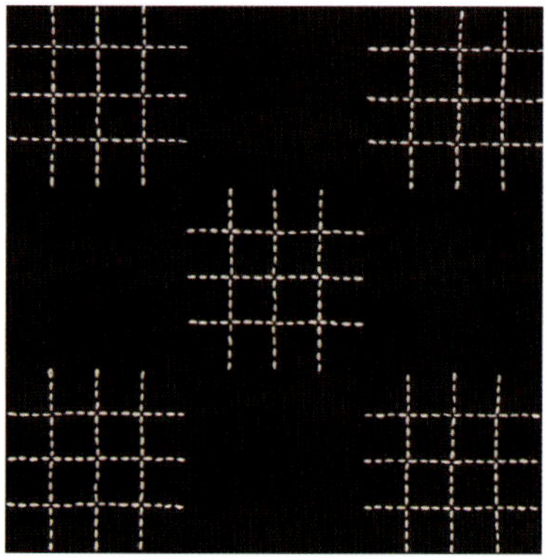

This simple design resembles kasuri ikat patterns.

Stitching the sashiko

Cut out a 9½ in. (24 cm) square of fabric and mark a ¼ in. (6 mm) seam allowance all around it. Mark a 3 in. (7.6 cm) base grid onto the central square, then subdivide alternate squares with a ¾ in. (1.9 cm) grid. Following the red arrows on the diagram, stitch the vertical lines first, keeping the thread continuous and stranding across the back where indicated by dashed lines. Stitch the horizontal rows in the same way, taking care not to stitch through the vertical strands on the back. Refer to pages 40–41 for tips on sashiko stitching.

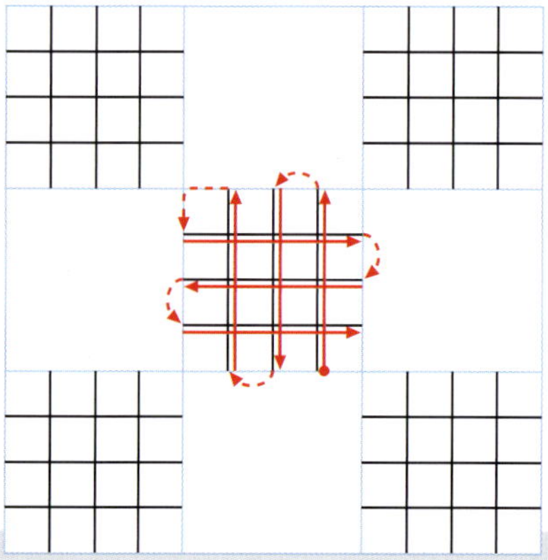

88 Kagome

(Bamboo basket)

This easy pattern resembles basketweave.

Stitching the sashiko

Cut out a 9½ in. (24 cm) square of fabric and mark a ¼ in. (6 mm) seam allowance all around it. Mark a ¾ x 1½ in. (1.9 x 3.8 cm) base grid onto the central square, then mark the sashiko design. Following the red arrow on the diagram, stitch the vertical lines. Follow the blue and green arrows to stitch diagonal lines. Refer to pages 40–41 for tips on sashiko stitching.

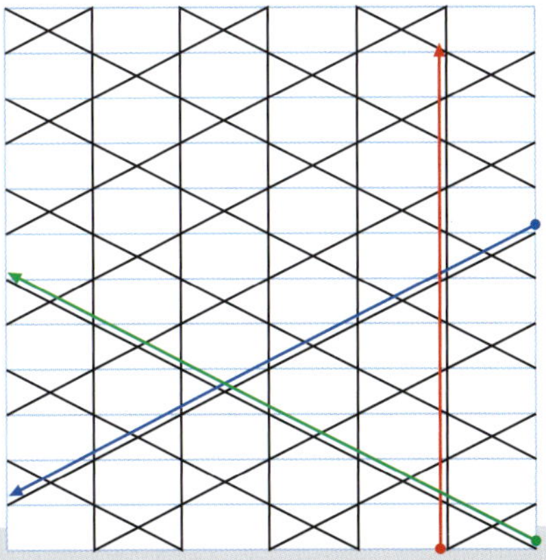

89 Seigaiha

(Blue ocean waves)

This cool and refreshing pattern dates from the 18th century.

Stitching the sashiko

Cut out a 9½ in. (24 cm) square of fabric and mark a ¼ in. (6 mm) seam allowance all around it. Mark a 1½ in. (3.8 cm) base grid onto the central square. Use 3-in. (7.6-cm) and 2½-in. (6.4-cm) diameter circle templates to mark the sashiko design. Following the red arrows on the diagram, stitch the largest arcs first, working in rows from the bottom upwards. Follow the blue and green arrows to stitch the inner and lower arcs, working in rows and stranding across the back where indicated by dashed lines. Refer to pages 40–41 for tips on sashiko stitching.

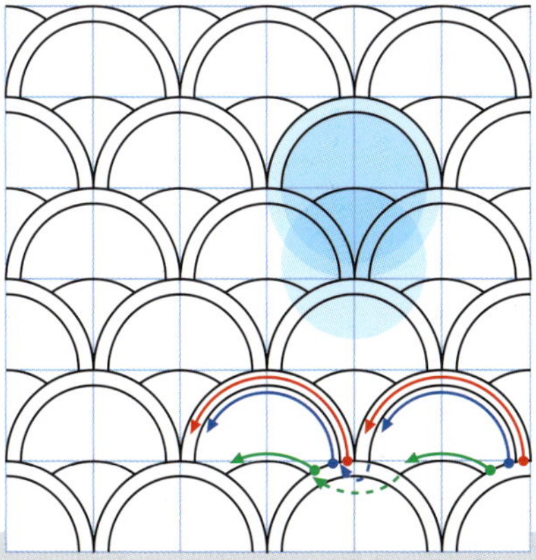

90 Nowaki

("Grasses")

Nowaki means 'wintry blast', representing the autumn wind through grass.

Stitching the sashiko

Cut out a 9½ in. (24 cm) square of fabric and mark a ¼ in. (6 mm) seam allowance all around it. Mark a 1½ in. (3.8 cm) base grid onto the central square. Use a 3-in. (7.6-cm) diameter circle template to mark the arcs. Use the same template to mark the curved 'grasses', pivoting the template against the grid intersection point. Following the red arrows on the diagram, stitch across each row. Start by stitching the lower 'grass' first, then strand across the back to stitch the upper 'grass', and finally stitch across the arc. Repeat to the end of each row. Refer to pages 40–41 for tips on sashiko stitching.

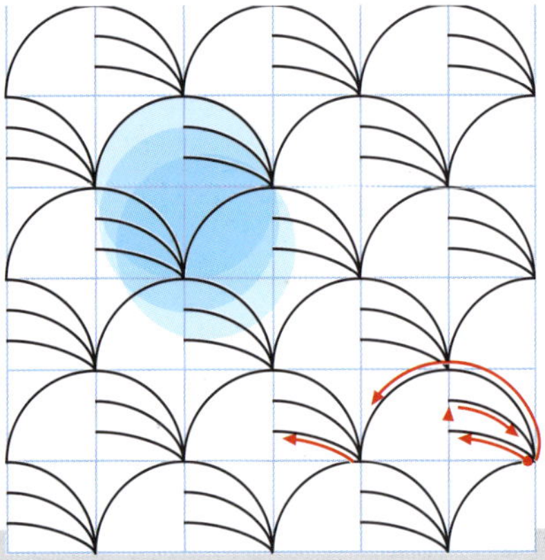

91 Chidori tsunagi

(Linked plovers)

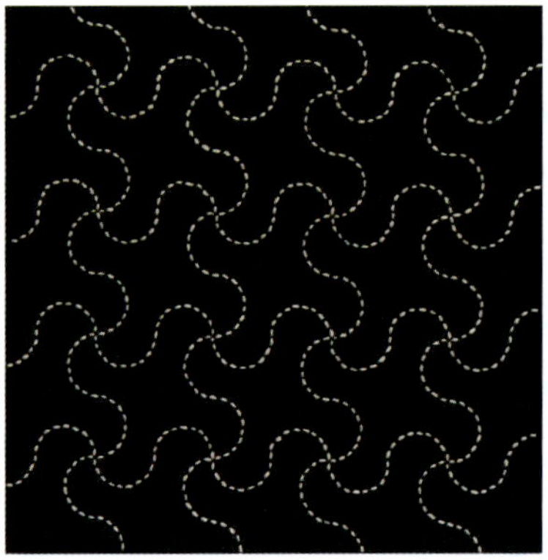

Cute little bird shapes interlock for this design.

Stitching the sashiko

Cut out a 9½ in. (24 cm) square of fabric and mark a ¼ in. (6 mm) seam allowance all around it. Mark a 1 in. (2.5 cm) base grid onto the central square, but place the outer lines ½ in. (1.3 cm) from the edge so that the design will be centred on the block. Use a 1-in. (2.5-cm) diameter circle template to mark the sashiko design. Following the red and then blue arrows on the diagram, stitch the vertical and then horizontal wavy lines. Refer to pages 40–41 for tips on sashiko stitching.

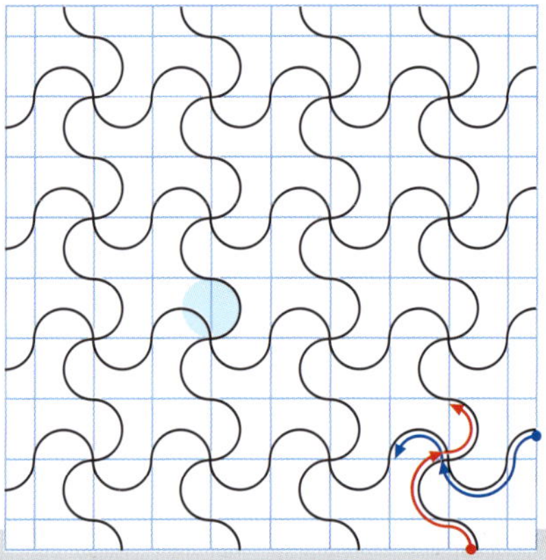

92 Amimon

(Net)

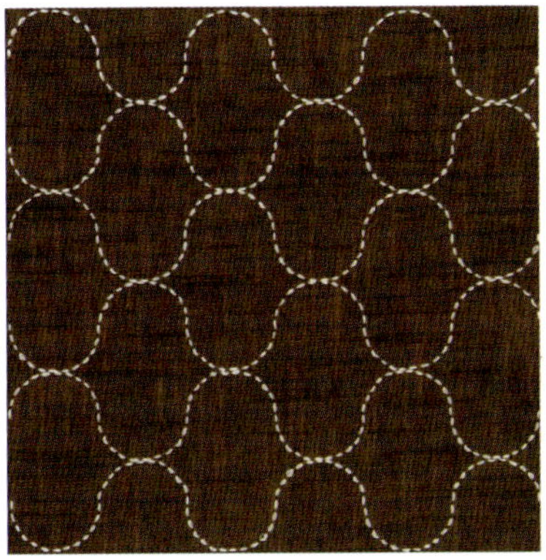

Fishing nets are an auspicious pattern, associated with a great catch.

Stitching the sashiko

Cut out a 9½ in. (24 cm) square of fabric and mark a ¼ in. (6 mm) seam allowance all around it. Mark a 1½ in. (3.8 cm) base grid onto the central square. Use a 1½-in. (3.8-cm) diameter circle template to mark the sashiko design. Following the red and then blue arrows on the diagram, stitch the horizontal wavy lines. Refer to pages 40–41 for tips on sashiko stitching.

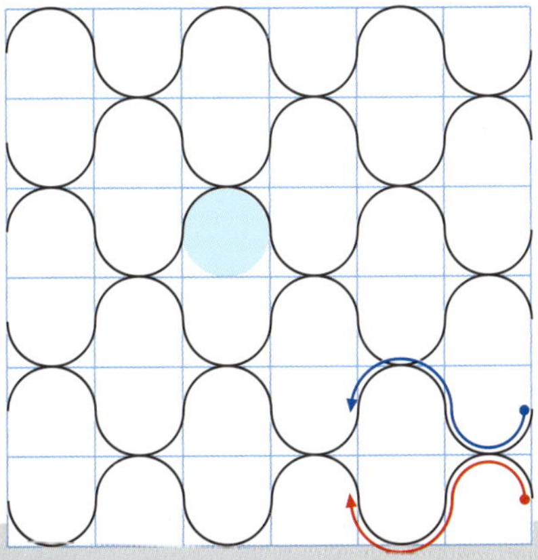

93 Yabane

(Arrows)

The arrow has been a traditional symbol of the warrior from the earliest times.

Stitching the sashiko

Cut out a 9½ in. (24 cm) square of fabric and mark a ¼ in. (6 mm) seam allowance all around it. Mark a 1½ in. (3.8 cm) base grid onto the central square, then mark the sashiko design. Following the red arrow on the diagram, stitch each of the step patterns. Following the blue arrows, stitch the short diagonal lines, keeping the thread continuous and stranding across the back where indicated by dashed lines. Refer to pages 40–41 for tips on sashiko stitching.

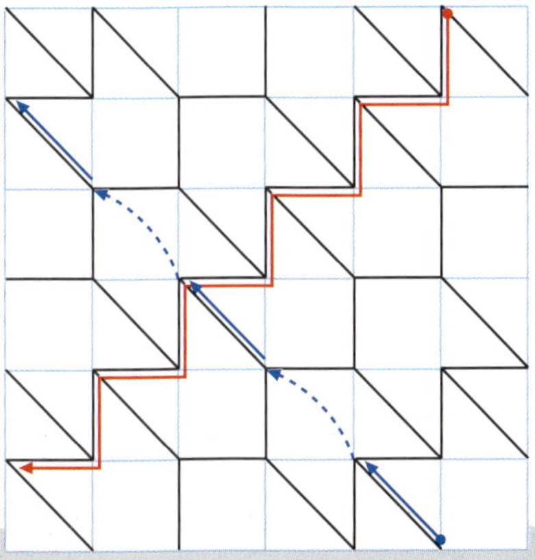

94 Hiragumi manji tsunagi

(Linked Buddhist symbols)

An ancient Buddhist symbol from India, manji signifies life and the universe.

Stitching the sashiko

Cut out a 9½ in. (24 cm) square of fabric and mark a ¼ in. (6 mm) seam allowance all around it. Mark a 1½ in. (3.8 cm) base grid onto the central square, then mark the sashiko design. Following the red arrows on the diagram, stitch the vertical sections of the pattern, keeping the thread continuous and stranding across the back where indicated by dashed lines. Follow the blue arrows to stitch the horizontal sections of the pattern. Refer to pags 40–41 for tips on sashiko stitching.

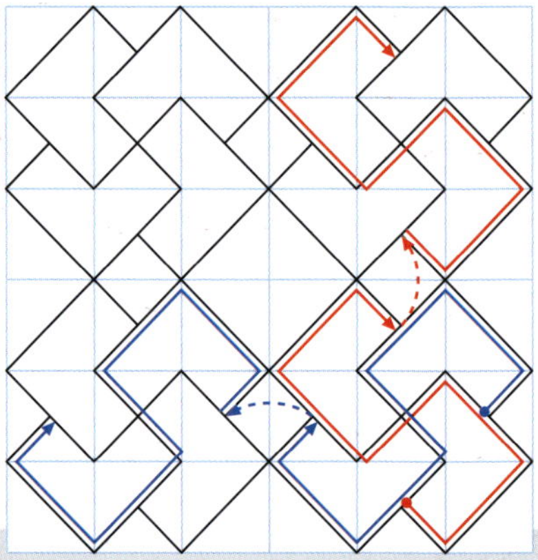

95 Higaki

(Cypress fence)

This pattern is popular both as a rinzu (silk damask) pattern for women's kimono and for woven fences.

Stitching the sashiko

Cut out a 9½ in. (24 cm) square of fabric and mark a ¼ in. (6 mm) seam allowance all around it. Mark a ¾ in. (1.9 cm) base grid onto the central square, then mark the sashiko design. Following the red arrows on the diagram, stitch the pattern in vertical sections, keeping the thread continuous and stranding across the back where indicated by dashed lines. Refer to pages 40–41 for tips on sashiko stitching.

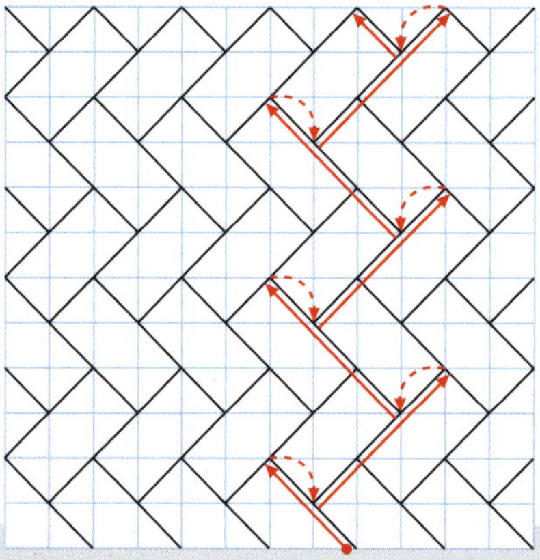

96 Yatsude asanoha

(Eight-lobed hemp leaf)

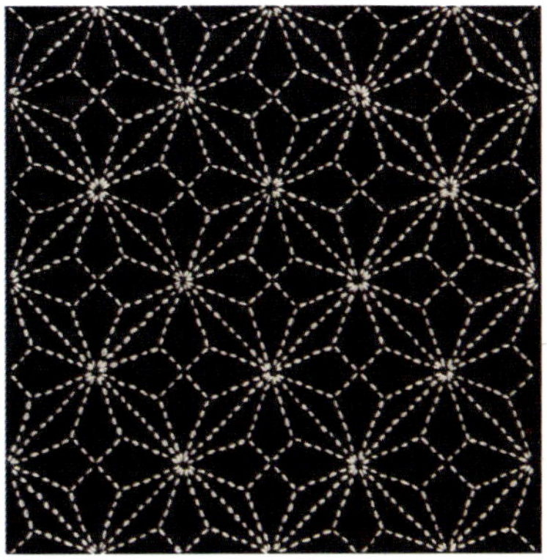

This pattern, based on the Fatsia japonica *leaf, was stitched to protect the wearer.*

Stitching the sashiko

Cut out a 9½ in. (24 cm) square of fabric and mark a ¼ in. (6 mm) seam allowance all around it. Mark a 1½ in. (3.8 cm) base grid onto the central square, then mark the sashiko design. Note that subdividing each square of the grid vertically and horizontally by 4 will help you to mark the design with accuracy. Following the red and blue arrows on the diagram, stitch the long diagonal lines. Following the green arrows, stitch the shallow zigzags in continuous lines. Following the pink arrow, stitch the short diagonal lines, stranding across the back where indicated by dashed lines. Refer to pages 40–41 for tips on sashiko stitching.

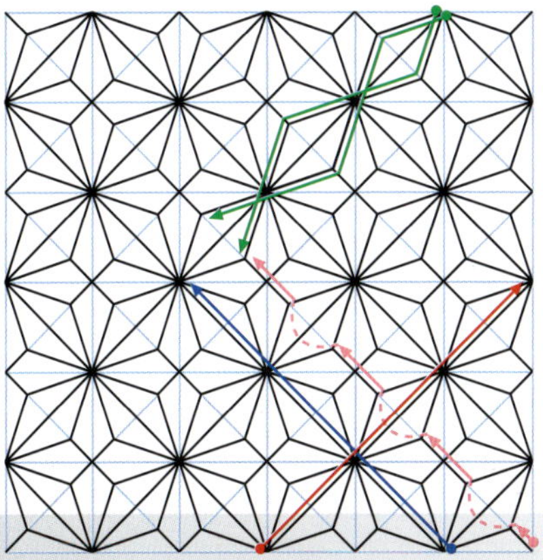

Mix & Match

ideas for combining blocks

Above, from top left: 15 x block 95; 1 each x blocks 108, 105, 112, 111 and 106 (2nd column); 1 each x blocks 110, 109, 103, 113 and 107 (4th column). Below, from top left: 13 x block 94; 12 x block 119.

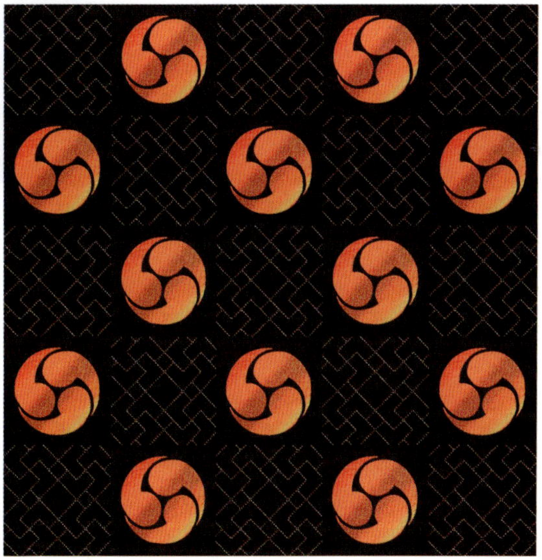

97 Asanoha

(Hemp leaf)

Associated particularly with babies and children, asanoha was stitched for protection.

Stitching the sashiko

Cut out a 9½ in. (24 cm) square of fabric and mark a ¼ in. (6 mm) seam allowance all around it. Mark a 1½ x ¾ in. (3.8 x 1.9 cm) base grid onto the central square, then mark the sashiko design. Note that subdividing each rectangle of the grid vertically by 4 will help you to mark the design with accuracy. Following the red arrow on the diagram, stitch the vertical lines. Following the blue arrows, stitch the wide zigzags to form figure-of-eights. Following the green arrows, stitch the shallow zigzags, also forming figure-of-eights. Following the pink arrows, stitch the horizontal lines, keeping the thread continuous and stranding across the back where indicated by dashed lines. Refer to pages 40–41 for tips on sashiko stitching.

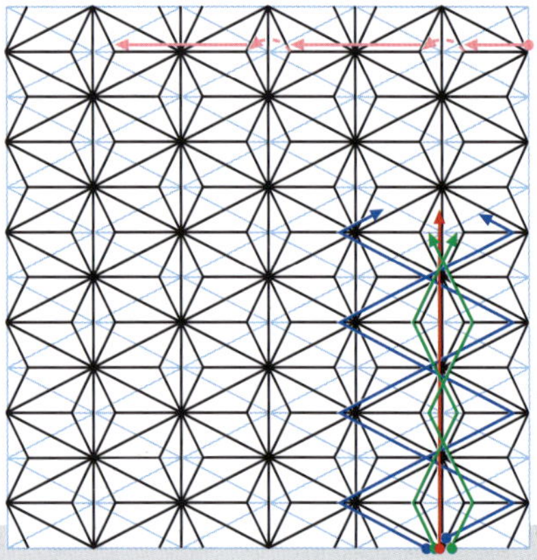

98 Sayagata

(Saya brocade pattern)

This brocade pattern came to Japan via the Silk Route over 600 years ago.

Stitching the sashiko

Cut out a 9½ in. (24 cm) square of fabric and mark a ¼ in. (6 mm) seam allowance all around it. Mark a ½ x 1 in. (1.2 x 2.5 cm) base grid onto the central square, then mark the sashiko design. Following the red and then the blue arrows on the diagram, stitch the first diagonal line in the centre of the block, then work around the pattern. Keep the maze-like diagram in front of you while you work to ensure you stitch it correctly. Refer to pages 40–41 for tips on sashiko stitching.

99 Kikkō hishi tsunagi

(Linked diamond tortoiseshell)

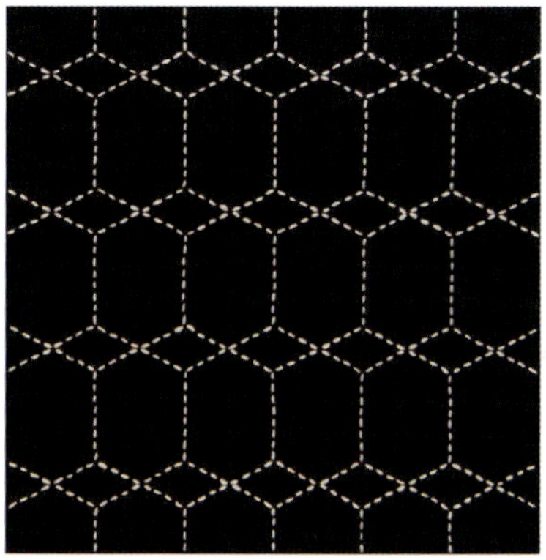

This pattern is also known as kasane kikkō (layered tortoiseshell), because the hexagons overlap.

Stitching the sashiko

Cut out a 9½ in. (24 cm) square of fabric and mark a ¼ in. (6 mm) seam allowance all around it. Mark a ¾ x 1½ in. (1.9 x 3.8 cm) base grid onto the central square, then mark the sashiko design. Following the red and then the blue arrows on the diagram, stitch the horizontal zigzag lines. Following the green arrows, stitch the remaining vertical lines, keeping the thread continuous and stranding across the back where indicated by dashed lines. Refer to pages 40–41 for tips on sashiko stitching.

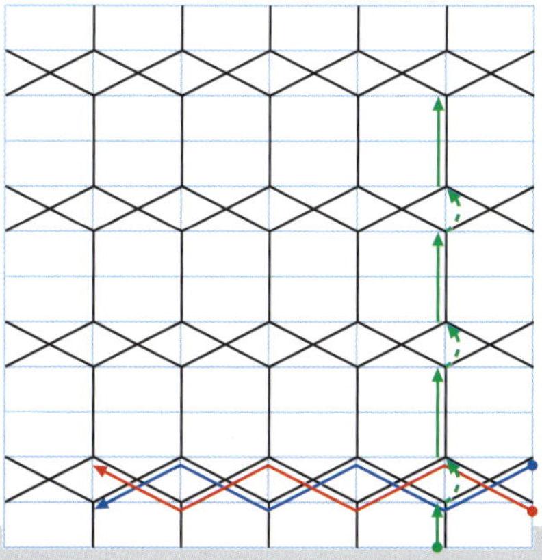

100 Musubi kikkō

(Connected tortoiseshell)

This pattern is easier to stitch than it looks, combining lucky threes with hexagons for longevity.

Stitching the sashiko

Cut out a 9½ in. (24 cm) square of fabric and mark a ¼ in. (6 mm) seam allowance all around it. Mark a ¾ x 1½ in. (1.9 x 3.8 cm) base grid onto the central square, then mark the sashiko design. Following the red arrows on the diagram, stitch the vertical lines. Following the blue and then the green arrows, stitch the diagonal lines. Keep the thread continuous for all the lines, stranding across the back where indicated by dashed lines. Refer to pages 40–41 for tips on sashiko stitching.

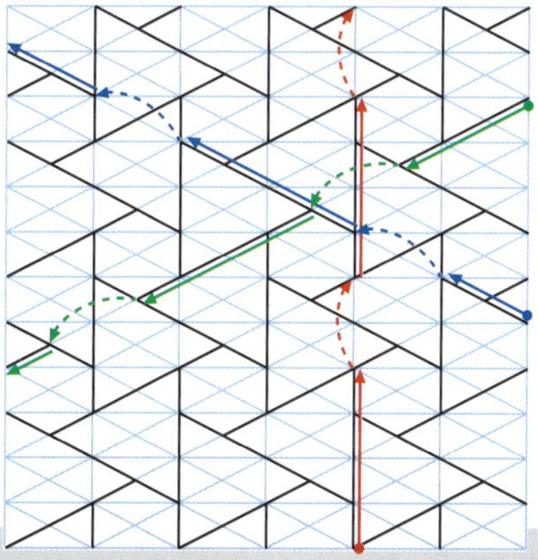

101 Matsukawabishi

(Pine bark diamond)

Pine represents long life and good fortune.

Stitching the sashiko

Cut out a 9½ in. (24 cm) square of fabric and mark a ¼ in. (6 mm) seam allowance all around it. Mark a ¾ x 1½ in. (1.9 x 3.8 cm) base grid onto the central square, but place the outer vertical lines ¾ in. (1.9 cm) from the edge so that the design will be centred on the block. Then mark the sashiko design. Following the red and blue arrows on the diagram, stitch the pattern in continuous lines. Refer to pages 40–41 for tips on sashiko stitching.

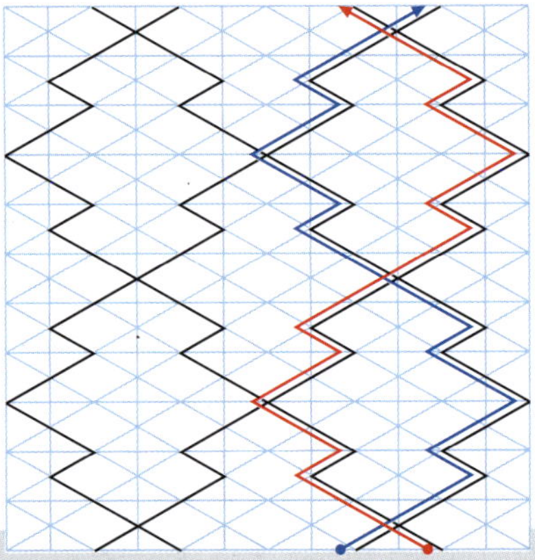

102 Yamagata

(Mountain form)

In Japanese tradition, mountains are the home of the gods.

Stitching the sashiko

Cut out a 9½ in. (24 cm) square of fabric and mark a ¼ in. (6 mm) seam allowance all around it. Mark a ¾ x 1½ in. (1.9 x 3.8 cm) base grid onto the central square, then mark the sashiko design. Following the red arrow on the diagram, stitch the zigzag lines. Following the blue arrow, stitch the stepped lines. Refer to pages 40–41 for tips on sashiko stitching.

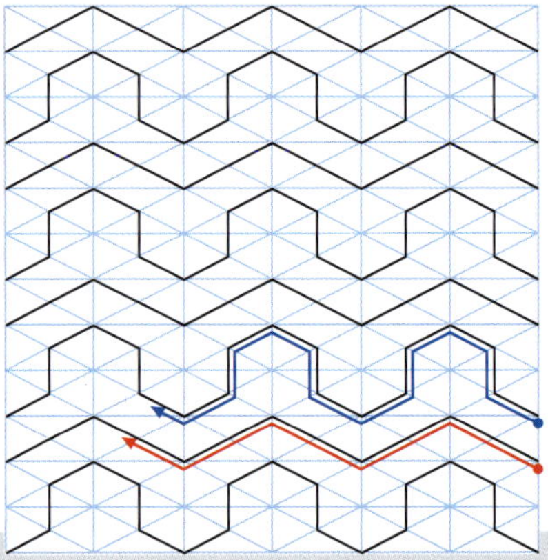

103 Tomoe ume

(Comma-style plum blossom)

To appliqué the crest, cut fabric pieces for the areas indicated with solid lines on the diagram.

Stitching the crest

Cut out a 9½ in. (24 cm) square of fabric. Enlarge the diagram by 250% and transfer the pattern onto the square, making sure it is centred. Stitch around the pattern, starting with the centre circle and then each petal. Refer to pages 40–41 for tips on sashiko stitching.

104 Tsuta

(Ivy leaf)

To appliqué the crest, cut fabric pieces for the areas indicated with solid lines on the diagram. Add running stitch details for the dashed lines.

Stitching the crest

Cut out a 9½ in. (24 cm) square of fabric. Enlarge the diagram by 250% and transfer the pattern onto the square, making sure it is centred. Stitch around the pattern, starting with the leaf outlines and then the veins. Refer to pages 40–41 for tips on sashiko stitching.

105 Yama

(Mountain)

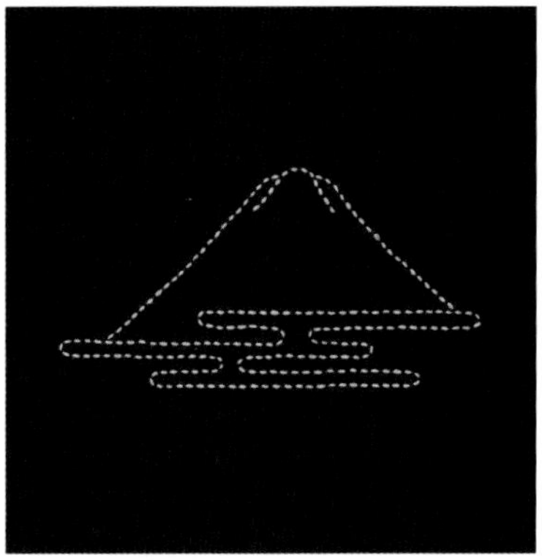

To appliqué the crest, cut fabric pieces for the areas indicated with solid lines on the diagram. Add running stitch details for the dashed lines.

Stitching the crest

Cut out a 9½ in. (24 cm) square of fabric. Enlarge the diagram by 250% and transfer the pattern onto the square, making sure it is centred. Stitch around the pattern, starting with the misty cloud. Refer to pages 40–41 for tips on sashiko stitching.

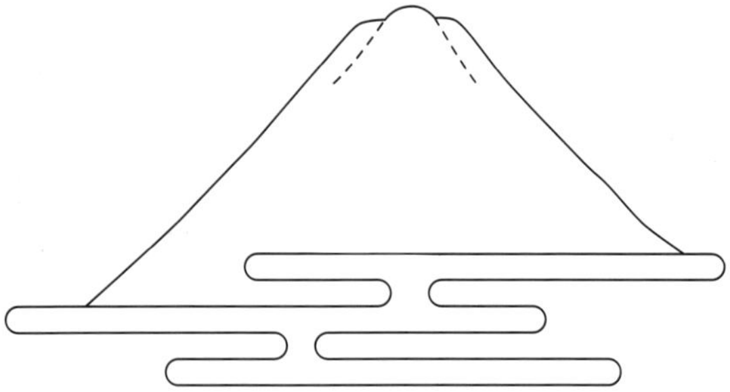

106 Mitsu ichō

(Three ginkgo leaves)

To appliqué the crest, cut fabric pieces for the areas indicated with solid lines on the diagram, overlapping the leaf stalks. Add running stitch details for the dashed lines.

Stitching the crest

Cut out a 9½ in. (24 cm) square of fabric. Enlarge the diagram by 250% and transfer the pattern onto the square, making sure it is centred. Stitch around the pattern, starting with the outside of the first leaf. Refer to pages 40–41 for tips on sashiko stitching.

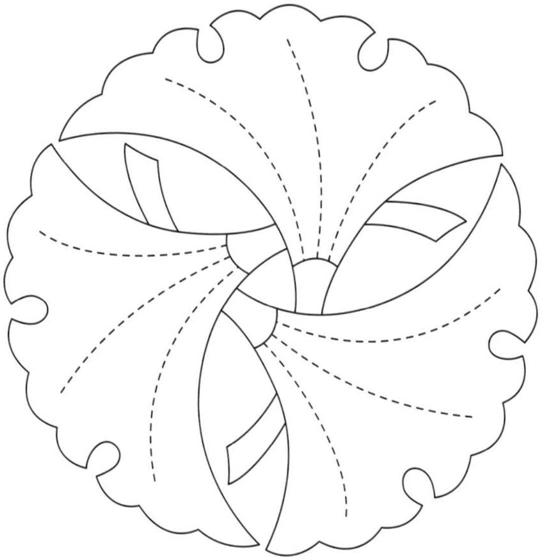

107 Nami

(Wave)

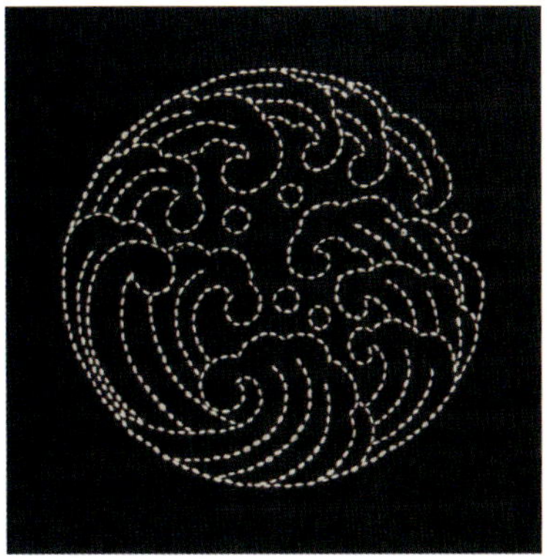

To appliqué the crest, cut fabric pieces for the areas indicated with solid lines on the diagram. Add running stitch details for the dashed lines. You could cut the waves in sections if you prefer, using a shaded fabric to suggest the crests of the waves.

Stitching the crest

Cut out a 9½ in. (24 cm) square of fabric. Enlarge the diagram by 250% and transfer the pattern onto the square, making sure it is centred. Stitch around the pattern, starting with the outline of the lowest wave. Refer to pages 40–41 for tips on sashiko stitching.

Mix & Match

ideas for combining blocks

Above, from top left: 8 x block 14; 1 each x blocks 103, 105, 108, 107, 106, 112 and 104.

108 Yukimochi sasa

(Bamboo with snowflake)

To appliqué the crest, cut fabric pieces for the areas indicated with solid lines on the diagram. Add running stitch details for the dashed lines. For a natural effect, use striped fabric for the bamboo leaves.

Stitching the crest

Cut out a 9½ in. (24 cm) square of fabric. Enlarge the diagram by 250% and transfer the pattern onto the square, making sure it is centred. Stitch around the pattern, starting with the outline of the lowest leaf. Refer to pages 40–41 for tips on sashiko stitching.

109 Karabana

(Imaginary Chinese flower)

To appliqué the crest, cut fabric pieces for the areas indicated with solid lines on the diagram. Add running stitch details for the dashed lines. Use one fabric for the petals and circle and another for the sword blades.

Stitching the crest

Cut out a 9½ in. (24 cm) square of fabric. Enlarge the diagram by 250% and transfer the pattern onto the square, making sure it is centred. Stitch around the pattern, starting with the centre circle and then stitching around each petal and sword blade. Refer to pages 40–41 for tips on sashiko stitching.

110 Kiri

(Paulownia flowers and leaf)

To appliqué the crest, cut fabric pieces for the areas indicated with solid lines on the diagram. Add running stitch details for the dashed lines. Use shaded or marbled fabrics for naturalistic leaves.

Stitching the crest

Cut out a 9½ in. (24 cm) square of fabric. Enlarge the diagram by 250% and transfer the pattern onto the square, making sure it is centred. Stitch around the pattern, starting with the outline of the lowest leaf. Refer to pages 40–41 for tips on sashiko stitching.

111 Tsuki ni kumo

(Moon)

To appliqué the crest, cut fabric pieces for the areas indicated with solid lines on the diagram. Use pale fabric for the moon to increase its brilliance.

Stitching the crest

Cut out a 9½ in. (24 cm) square of fabric. Enlarge the diagram by 250% and transfer the pattern onto the square, making sure it is centred. Stitch around the pattern, starting with the outline of the lowest cloud. Refer to pages 40–41 for tips on sashiko stitching.

112 Tachibana

(Japanese orange blossom)

To appliqué the crest, cut fabric pieces for the areas indicated with solid lines on the diagram. Add running stitch details for the dashed lines. Use the same fabric for the leaves below and behind the blossom.

Stitching the crest

Cut out a 9½ in. (24 cm) square of fabric. Enlarge the diagram by 250% and transfer the pattern onto the square, making sure it is centred. Stitch around the pattern, starting with the central blossom. Refer to pages 40–41 for tips on sashiko stitching.

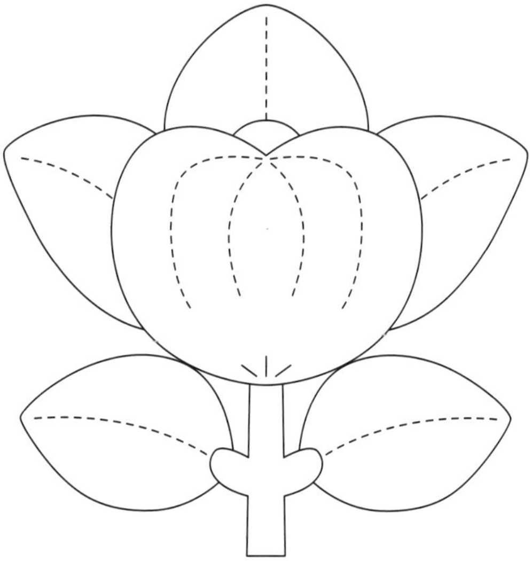

113 Maru tsuru

(Crane circle)

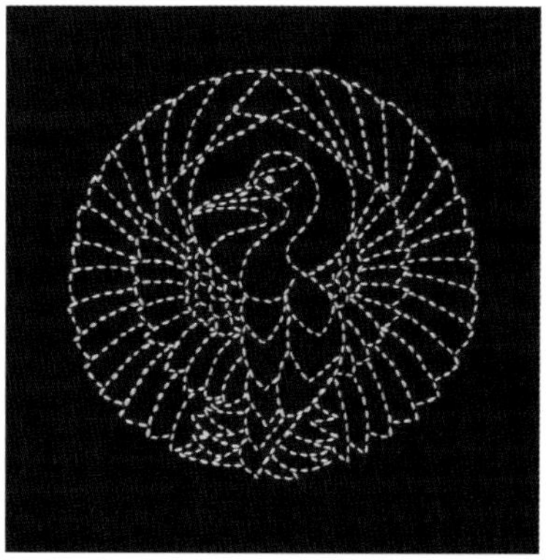

To appliqué the crest, cut fabric pieces for the areas indicated with solid lines on the diagram. Add running stitch details for the dashed lines. Use white and light grey fabric for the wings, black for the tail and graduate from black to white from head to body.

Stitching the crest

Cut out a 9½ in. (24 cm) square of fabric. Enlarge the diagram by 250% and transfer the pattern onto the square, making sure it is centred. Stitch around the pattern, starting with the outline of the crane's body. Refer to pages 40–41 for tips on sashiko stitching.

114 Sakura

(Cherry blossom)

Omit the background circle if you wish. To make a sashiko crest, use the diagram to mark the design on the background fabric and then stitch all the lines, both solid and dashed.

CUTTING LIST

A
B
C
D

Enlarge the diagram by 200% and make templates for the crest, adding turning allowances if necessary when cutting out the fabric.

- A One 9½ in. (24 cm) square, with a 7-in. (18-cm) diameter circle cut out from the centre.
- B One 8-in. (20.3-cm) diameter circle.
- C Five large petals.
- C One small centre circle.
- D Five small petals.

Construction

Piece the large circle into the square (page 36). Appliqué all the crest pieces to this background circle. Add running stitch details along the large petals as indicated by the dashed lines. Refer to pages 38–39 for tips on appliqué.

115 Mitsuho no maru

(Ship's sails)

Omit the background circle if you wish. To make a sashiko crest, use the diagram to mark the design on the background fabric and then stitch all the lines, both solid and dashed.

CUTTING LIST

Enlarge the diagram by 200% and make templates for the crest, adding turning allowances if necessary when cutting out the fabric.

- A One 9½ in. (24 cm) square, with a 7-in. (18-cm) diameter circle cut out from the centre.
- B One 8-in. (20.3-cm) diameter circle.
- C Five sails.
- D About 1 yd. (1 m) of ¼-in. (6-mm) wide fusible bias tape.

Construction

Piece the large circle into the square (page 36). Appliqué the sails to this background circle, leaving the straight edges raw. Appliqué the bias tape in place, starting with the two sloping pieces, then the vertical mast, then the two horizontal pieces. Add running stitch details along the sails as indicated by the dashed lines. Refer to pages 38–39 for tips on appliqué.

116 Mitsuya

(Three arrows)

Cut the pairs of feathers with symmetrical stripes angled towards the centre. Omit the background circle if you wish. To make a sashiko crest, use the diagram to mark the design on the background fabric and then stitch all the lines, both solid and dashed.

CUTTING LIST

A 
B 
C 
D 
E 

Enlarge the diagram by 200% and make templates for the crest, adding turning allowances if necessary when cutting out the fabric.

- A One 9½ in. (24 cm) square, with a 7-in. (18-cm) diameter circle cut out from the centre.
- B One 8-in. (20.3-cm) diameter circle.
- C Three pairs of arrow feathers.
- D One small centre circle.
- E About 1 ft. (30 cm) of ¼-in. (6-mm) wide fusible bias tape.

Construction

Piece the large circle into the square (page 36). Appliqué the arrow feathers to this background circle, leaving the inside edges raw and making sure they will be covered by bias tape. Appliqué the bias tape in place, then the centre circle. Add running stitch details along the feathers as indicated by the dashed lines. Refer to pages 38–39 for tips on appliqué.

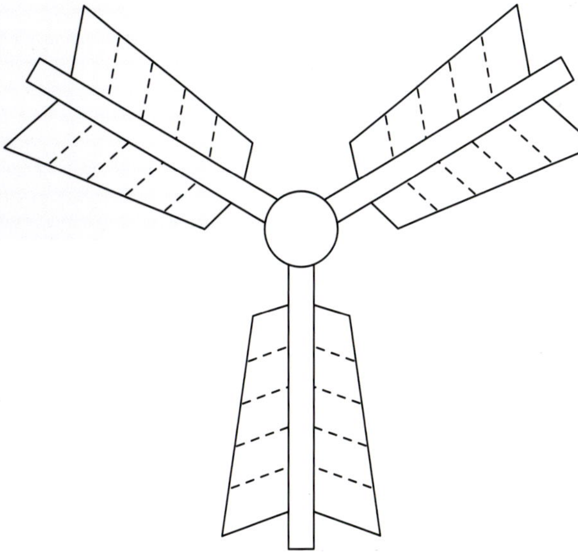

Mix & Match

ideas for combining blocks

Above, from top left: 4 x block 114; 8 x block 51; 2 x block; 2 x block 116.

117 Ōgi

(Folding fan)

Omit the background circle if you wish. To make a sashiko crest, use the diagram to mark the design on the background fabric and then stitch all the lines, both solid and dashed.

CUTTING LIST

Enlarge the diagram by 200% and make templates for the crest, adding turning allowances if necessary when cutting out the fabric.

- A One 9½ in. (24 cm) square, with a 7-in. (18-cm) diameter circle cut out from the centre.
- B One 8-in. (20.3-cm) diameter circle.
- C One fan paper.
- D About 1 yd. (1 m) of ¼-in. (6-mm) wide fusible bias tape.

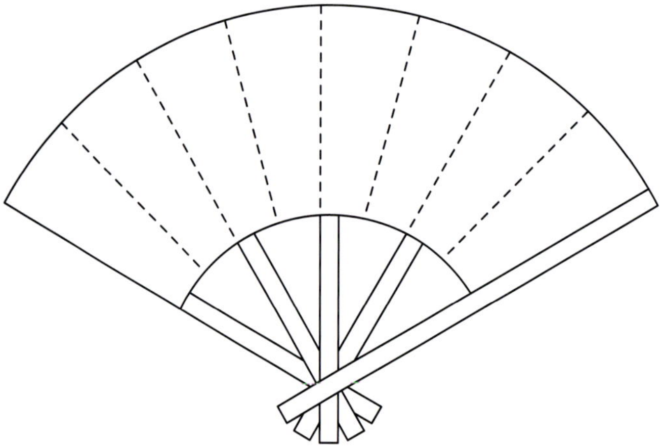

Construction

Piece the large circle into the square (page 36). Appliqué the fan paper to this background circle, leaving the right edge raw. Appliqué the bias tape in place, starting with the four short fan sticks and making sure that the final long fan stick covers the raw edge of the fan paper. Add running stitch details along the fan paper as indicated by the dashed lines. Refer to pages 38–39 for tips on appliqué.

118 Genji guruma

(Carriage wheel)

To make a sashiko crest, use the diagram to mark the design on the background fabric and then stitch all the lines.

CUTTING LIST

A
B

Enlarge the diagram by 200% and make templates for the crest, adding turning allowances if necessary when cutting out the fabric.

A One 9½ in. (24 cm) square.
B Six outer wheel rims.
B Six inner wheel rims.
B Six wheel spokes.
B One small centre circle.

Construction

Appliqué all the pieces to the background square. Refer to pages 38–39 for tips on appliqué.

119 Tomoe

(Comma or whorl)

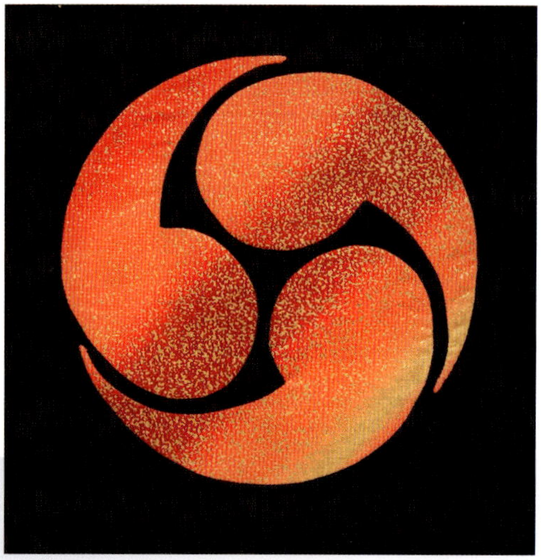

To make a sashiko crest, use the diagram to mark the design on the background fabric and then stitch all the lines.

CUTTING LIST

A
B

Enlarge the diagram by 200% and make templates for the crest, adding turning allowances if necessary when cutting out the fabric.

A One 9½ in. (24 cm) square.

B Three commas, either cut separately or from a single piece of fabric so that the pattern flows across them.

Construction

Appliqué all the pieces to the background square. Refer to pages 38–39 for tips on appliqué.

120 Mitsu ume

(Three plum blossoms)

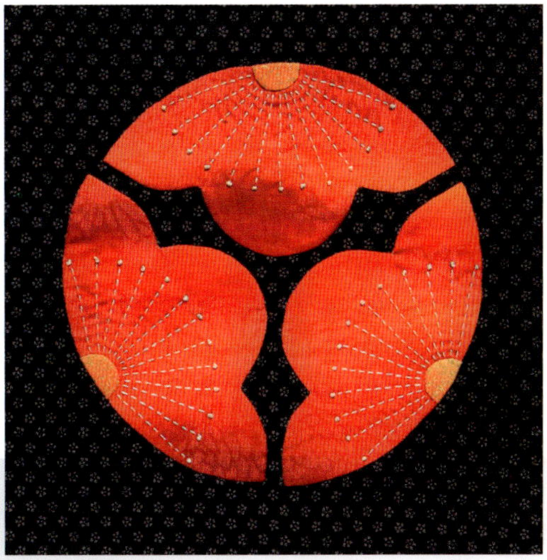

To make a sashiko crest, use the diagram to mark the design on the background fabric and then stitch all the lines, both solid and dashed.

CUTTING LIST

A 

B 

C 

Enlarge the diagram by 200% and make templates for the crest, adding turning allowances if necessary when cutting out the fabric.

A One 9½ in. (24 cm) square.

B Three blossoms, either cut separately or from a single piece of fabric so that the pattern flows across them.

C Three blossom centres.

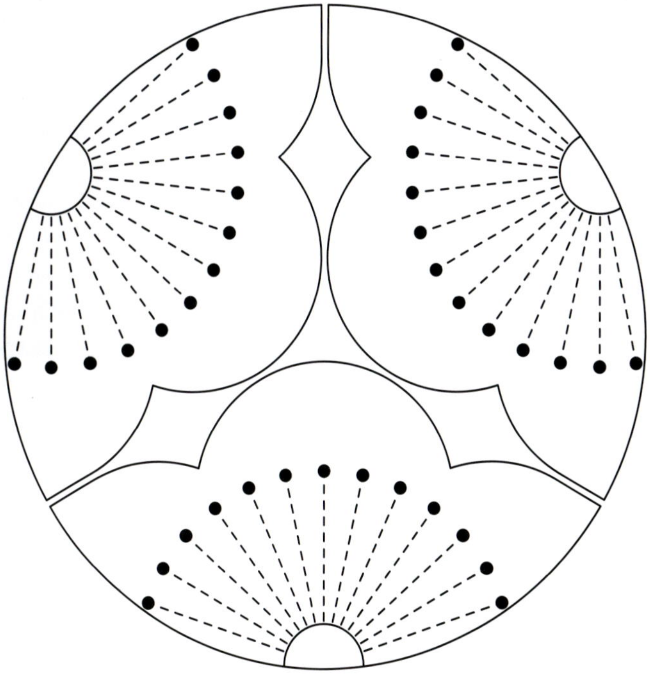

Construction

Appliqué all the pieces to the background square. Add running stitch details along the blossoms as indicated by the dashed lines, ending each line with a French knot as indicated by the black dots. Refer to pages 38–39 for tips on appliqué.

121 Kikkō tsuru

(Crane hexagon)

To make a sashiko crest, use the diagram to mark the design on the background fabric and then stitch all the lines.

CUTTING LIST

A

B

Enlarge the diagram by 200% and make templates for the crest, adding turning allowances if necessary when cutting out the fabric.

A One 9½ in. (24 cm) square.

B One crane hexagon, cut from a single piece of fabric so that the pattern flows across both sections.

Construction

Appliqué both pieces to the background square. Refer to pages 38–39 for tips on appliqué.

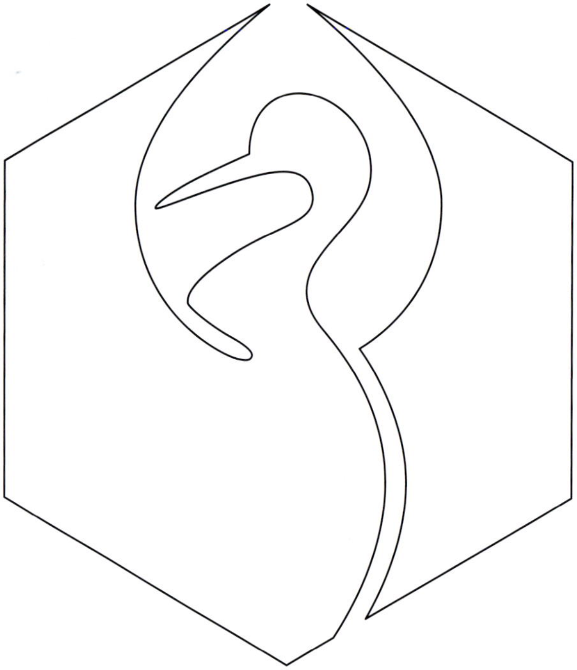

122 Mitsu fuji tomoe

(Triple wisteria whorl)

To make a sashiko crest, use the diagram to mark the design on the background fabric and then stitch all the lines, both solid and dashed.

Mix & Match

ideas for combining blocks

Above, from top left: 16 x block 97; 1 each x blocks 122, 117, 124, 118, 120, 125, 119, 121 and 123.

CUTTING LIST

A
B
C
D

Enlarge the diagram by 200% and make templates for the crest, adding turning allowances if necessary when cutting out the fabric.

- A One 9½ in. (24 cm) square.
- B Three wisteria racemes (each raceme is a single piece that extends beneath the bias strips). Cut them from a single piece of fabric so that the pattern flows across all three racemes.
- B Three flower tips.
- B One small circular bud.
- C Three leaves.
- D About 2 ft. (60 cm) of ¼-in. (6-mm) wide fusible bias tape.

Construction

Appliqué all the pieces and bias tape to the background square, easing the tape gently around the curves and overlapping the pieces to match the diagram. Any edges that are overlapped can be left raw. Add running stitch details along the wisteria racemes and leaves as indicated by the dashed lines. Refer to pages 38–39 for tips on appliqué.

123 Momiji

(Maple leaves)

To make a sashiko crest, use the diagram to mark the design on the background fabric and then stitch all the lines, both solid and dashed.

CUTTING LIST

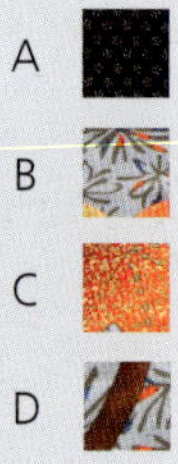

Enlarge the diagram by 200% and make templates for the crest, adding turning allowances if necessary when cutting out the fabric.

- A One 9½ in. (24 cm) square.
- B One 7½-in. (19-cm) diameter circle.
- C Five maple leaves in various sizes.
- D About 1 yd. (1 m) of ¼-in. (6-mm) wide fusible bias tape.

Construction

Appliqué all the pieces and bias tape to the background square, easing the tape gently around the curves and overlapping the pieces to match the diagram. Any edges that are overlapped, such as the large circle, can be left raw. Add running stitch details along the maple leaves as indicated by the dashed lines. Refer to pages 38–39 for tips on appliqué.

124 Matsu

(Pine tree)

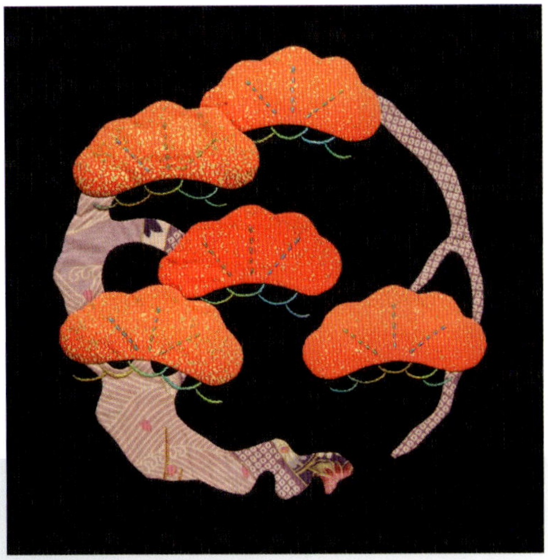

To make a sashiko crest, use the diagram to mark the design on the background fabric and then stitch all the lines, both solid and dashed.

CUTTING LIST

A
B
C

Enlarge the diagram by 200% and make templates for the crest, adding turning allowances if necessary when cutting out the fabric.

- A One 9½ in. (24 cm) square.
- B Tree trunk in three sections.
- C Five pine boughs.

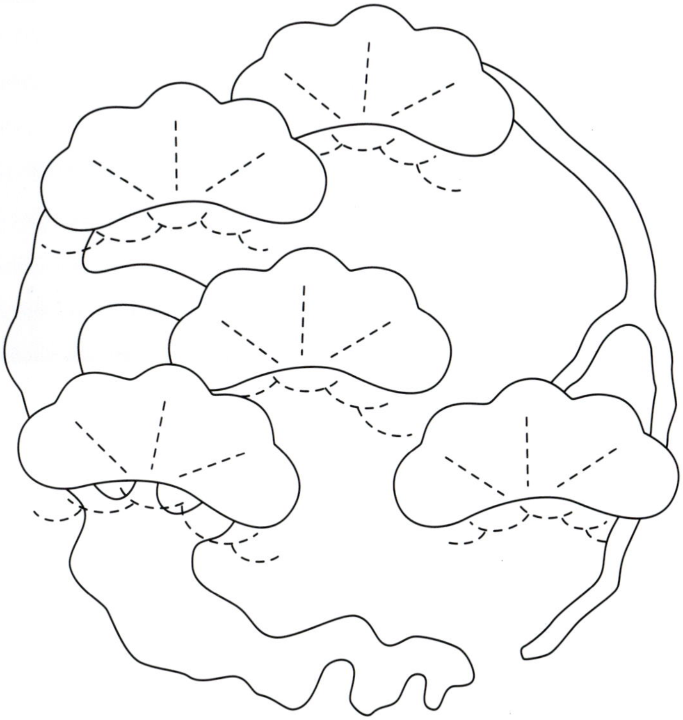

Construction

Appliqué all the pieces to the background square, overlapping them to match the diagram. Any edges that are overlapped can be left raw. Using the dashed lines on the diagram as a guide, add running stitch details inside the pine boughs and curved lines of stem stitch to form thin branches beneath the boughs. Refer to pages 38–39 for tips on appliqué.

125 Mukai chō

(Facing butterflies)

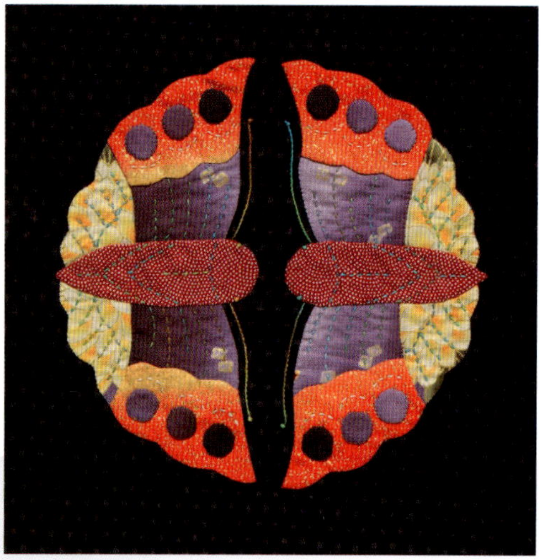

To make a sashiko crest, use the diagram to mark the design on the background fabric and then stitch all the lines, both solid and dashed.

CUTTING LIST

A
B
C
D
E

Enlarge the diagram by 200% and make templates for the crest, adding turning allowances if necessary when cutting out the fabric.

- A One 9½ in. (24 cm) square.
- B Two pairs of forewing centres.
- B Twelve small circles.
- C Two pairs of forewing edges.
- D Two pairs of hindwings.
- E Two bodies.

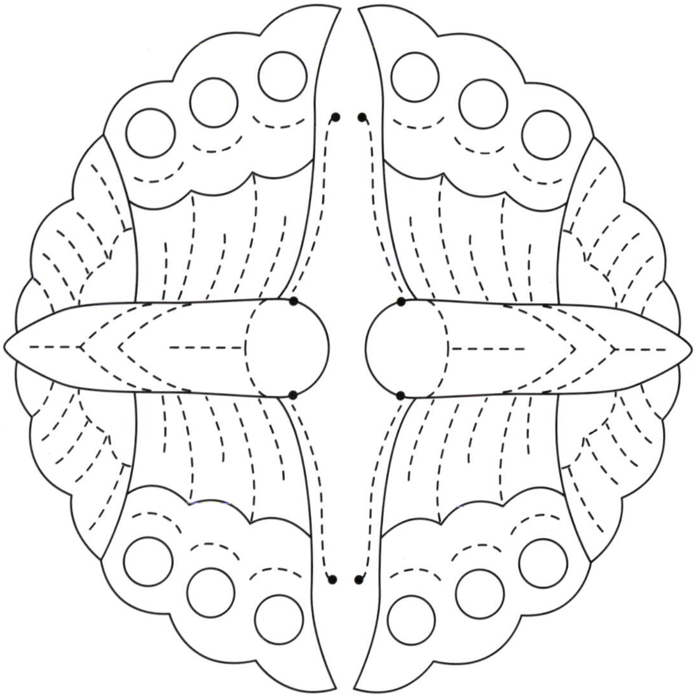

Construction

Appliqué all the pieces to the background square, overlapping them to match the diagram. Note that the forewings overlap the hindwings, and the forewing edges overlap the forewing centres. Any edges that are overlapped can be left raw. Using the dashed lines on the diagram as a guide, add running stitch details inside the butterflies, lines of stem stitch for antennae and French knots for eyes. Refer to pages 38–39 for tips on appliqué.

126 Hōjyu

(Wish-granting jewel)

Omit the background circle if you wish, but choose fabrics with greater contrast for the background square and symbol. To make a sashiko symbol, use the diagram to mark the design on the background fabric and then stitch all the lines.

CUTTING LIST

A 
B 
C 
D 

Enlarge the diagram by 200% and make templates for the crest, adding turning allowances if necessary when cutting out the fabric.

- A One 9½ in. (24 cm) square, with a 7-in. (18-cm) diameter circle cut out from the centre.
- B One 8-in. (20.3-cm) diameter circle.
- C One four-tiered jewel, cut from a single piece of fabric so that the pattern flows across all four sections.
- D One set of flames.

Construction

Piece the large circle into the square (page 36). Appliqué all the pieces to this background circle. If you find the repeated points of the flames difficult, use fusible appliqué for those. Refer to pages 38–39 for tips on appliqué.

127 Kakure gasa kakure mino

(Straw hat and cloak of invisibility)

Omit the background circle if you wish, but choose fabrics with greater contrast for the background square and symbol. To make a sashiko symbol, use the diagram to mark the design on the background fabric and then stitch all the lines, both solid and dashed.

CUTTING LIST

A 

B 

C 

D 

E 

F 

Enlarge the diagram by 200% and make templates for the crest, adding turning allowances if necessary when cutting out the fabric.

A One 9½ in. (24 cm) square, with a 7-in. (18-cm) diameter circle cut out from the centre.
B One 8-in. (20.3-cm) diameter circle.
C One oval hat.
D One hat tassel.
D One cloak.
E One collar.
E One small circle.
F About 2 ft. (60 cm) of ¼-in. (6-mm) wide fusible bias tape.

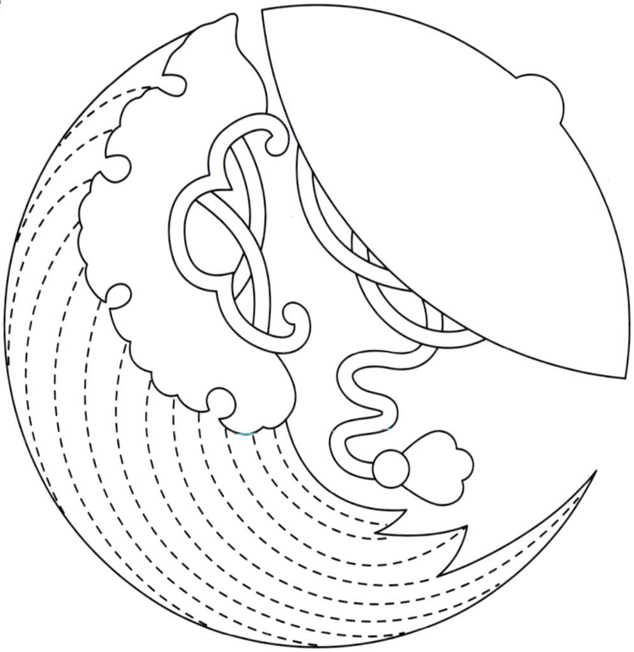

Construction

Piece the large circle into the square (page 36). Appliqué all the pieces and bias tape to this background circle, easing the tape gently around the curves and overlapping the pieces to match the diagram. Any edges that are overlapped can be left raw. Add running stitch details along the cloak as indicated by the dashed lines. Refer to pages 38–39 for tips on appliqué.

128 Kinchaku

(Treasure bag)

Omit the background circle if you wish, but choose fabrics with greater contrast for the background square and symbol. To make a sashiko symbol, use the diagram to mark the design on the background fabric and then stitch all the lines, both solid and dashed.

CUTTING LIST

A
B
C
D
E
F

Enlarge the diagram by 200% and make templates for the crest, adding turning allowances if necessary when cutting out the fabric.

- A One 9½ in. (24 cm) square, with a 7-in. (18-cm) diameter circle cut out from the centre.
- B One 8-in. (20.3-cm) diameter circle.
- C One bag.
- D Two tassels.
- E Two small circles.
- F About 2 ft. (60 cm) of ¼-in. (6-mm) wide fusible bias tape.

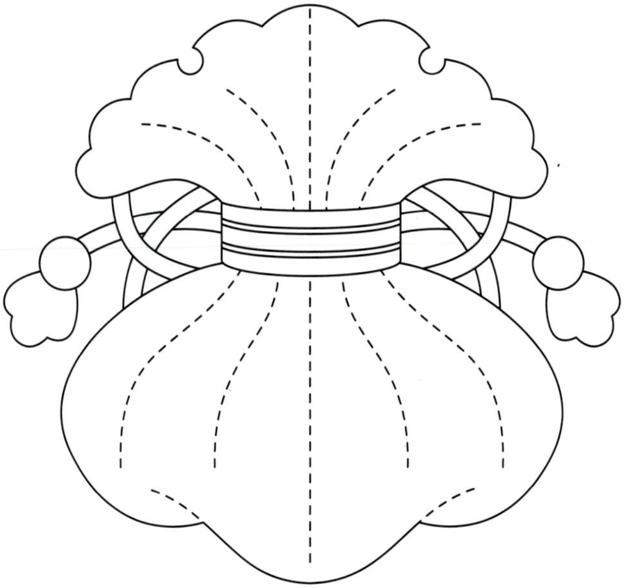

Construction

Piece the large circle into the square (page 36). Appliqué all the pieces and bias tape to this background circle, easing the tape gently around the curves and overlapping the pieces to match the diagram. Tuck in the ends of the bias tape around the neck of the bag. Add running stitch details along the bag as indicated by the dashed lines. Refer to pages 38–39 for tips on appliqué.

129 Noshi

('Increase' auspicious abalone bundle)

Omit the background circle if you wish, but choose fabrics with greater contrast for the background square and symbol. To make a sashiko symbol, use the diagram to mark the design on the background fabric and then stitch all the lines.

CUTTING LIST

Enlarge the diagram by 200% and make templates for the crest, adding turning allowances if necessary when cutting out the fabric.

- A One 9½ in. (24 cm) square, with a 7-in. (18-cm) diameter circle cut out from the centre.
- B One 8-in. (20.3-cm) diameter circle.
- C First strip (from top).
- D Second and fourth strip (from top).
- E Third and fifth strip (from top).
- F Two tassels.
- G Two small circles.
- E About 2 ft. (60 cm) of ¼-in. (6-mm) wide fusible bias tape.

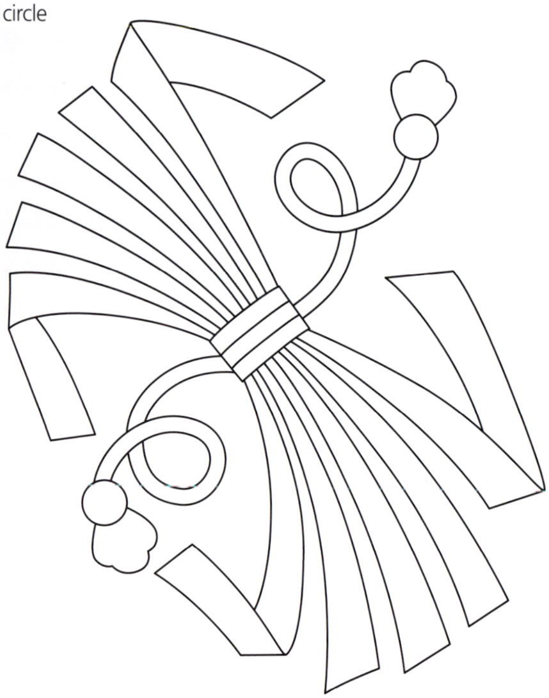

Construction

Piece the large circle into the square (page 36). Appliqué all the pieces and bias tape to this background circle, easing the tape gently around the curves and overlapping the pieces to match the diagram. Refer to pages 38–39 for tips on appliqué.

130 Hōyaku

(Treasure house key)

Omit the background circle if you wish, but choose fabrics with greater contrast for the background square and symbol. To make a sashiko symbol, use the diagram to mark the design on the background fabric and then stitch all the lines.

CUTTING LIST

Enlarge the diagram by 200% and make templates for the crest, adding turning allowances if necessary when cutting out the fabric.

- A One 9½ in. (24 cm) square, with a 7-in. (18-cm) diameter circle cut out from the centre.
- B One 8-in. (20.3-cm) diameter circle.
- C One key.
- D Two tassels.
- E Two small circles.
- F About 1 yd. (60 cm) of ¼-in. (6-mm) wide fusible bias tape.

Construction

Piece the large circle into the square (page 36). Appliqué all the pieces and bias tape to this background circle, easing the tape gently around the curves and overlapping the pieces to match the diagram. Refer to pages 38–39 for tips on appliqué.

Mix & Match

ideas for combining blocks

Above, from top left: 8 x block 84; 1 each x blocks 130, 128, 127, 132, 129, 131, 128 and 126.

131 Gunbai

(Referee's fan)

Omit the background circle if you wish, but choose fabrics with greater contrast for the background square and symbol. To make a sashiko symbol, use the diagram to mark the design on the background fabric and then stitch all the lines, both dashed and solid.

CUTTING LIST

A 

B 

C 

D 

E 

Enlarge the diagram by 200% and make templates for the crest, adding turning allowances if necessary when cutting out the fabric.

- A One 9½ in. (24 cm) square, with a 7-in. (18-cm) diameter circle cut out from the centre.
- A One tassel for top of fan stick.
- B One 8-in. (20.3-cm) diameter circle.
- C One fan (a single piece that extends beneath the fan stick).
- D Three fan decorations (each decoration should extend beneath the fan stick).
- D Two small circles.
- E About 1 yd. (1 m) of ¼-in. (6-mm) wide fusible bias tape.

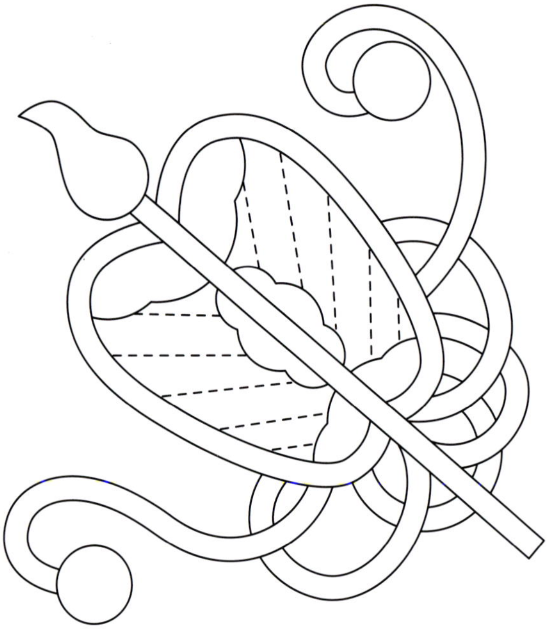

Construction

Piece the large circle into the square (page 36). Appliqué all the pieces and bias tape to this background circle, easing the tape gently around the curves and overlapping the pieces to match the diagram. Any edges that are overlapped can be left raw. Add running stitch details along the fan as indicated by the dashed lines. Refer to pages 38–39 for tips on appliqué.

132 Uchideno kozuchi

(Wish-granting mallet)

Omit the background circle if you wish, but choose fabrics with greater contrast for the background square and symbol. To make a sashiko symbol, use the diagram to mark the design on the background fabric and then stitch all the lines.

CUTTING LIST

Enlarge the diagram by 200% and make templates for the crest, adding turning allowances if necessary when cutting out the fabric.

- A The 9½ in. (24 cm) square, with a 7-in. (18-cm) diameter circle cut out from the centre.
- B One 8-in. (20.3-cm) diameter circle.
- C One main mallet head.
- C Two mallet side ovals (largest and smallest).
- D One mallet central cover.
- E One mallet side oval (middle size).
- E Two mallet handles.
- E Two small circles.
- F About 2 ft. (60 cm) of ¼-in. (6-mm) wide fusible bias tape.

Construction

Piece the large circle into the square (page 36). Appliqué all the pieces and bias tape to this background circle, easing the tape gently around the curves and overlapping the pieces to match the diagram. Note that part of the bias tape passes through the hole in the lower handle. Any edges that are overlapped can be left raw. Refer to pages 38–39 for tips on appliqué.

Index

Block index

Blocks are indexed by Japanese names, with English translations in parentheses. The Japanese names of patchwork blocks are in standard roman type; sashiko in *italic*; kamon in **bold**; and takarazukuchi in ***bold italic***. The numbers given are page numbers, not block numbers.

General index

Resources and Credits

Suppliers

JAPAN
Kimono Flea Market Ichiroya
Asia-Shoji Bldg. 301
1841-1 Nishi 1 chome
Wakamatsu cho Tondabayashi
Osaka 584-0025
info@ichiroya.com
www.ichiroya.com
Vintage kimono and textiles (webstore and mail order)

UNITED STATES
eQuilter.com
5455 Spine Road, Suite E
Boulder, CO 80301
Tel: USA Toll Free 877-FABRIC-3 or 303-527-0856
service@eQuilter.com
www.eQuilter.com
Fabrics and quilting supplies (mail order)

The Shibori Dragon
11124 Gravelly Lake Drive SW
Lakewood, WA 98499
Tel: (253) 582-7455
Fax: (253) 512-2323
shiboridragon@juno.com
www.shiboridragon.com
Japanese textiles and sashiko supplies (mail order)

AUSTRALIA
Sanshi
119 Solomon Street
Beaconsfield
Perth, WA 6162
Tel: (08) 9431 7336
info@sanshi.com.au
www.sanshi.com.au
Vintage and modern Japanese textiles (mail order)

UNITED KINGDOM
The Cotton Patch
1285 Stratford Road
Hall Green
Birmingham
West Midlands B28 9AJ
Tel: 0121 702 2840
mailorder@cottonpatch.net
www.cottonpatch.co.uk
Fabrics and quilting supplies (mail order and shop)

Euro Japan Links Ltd
32 Nant Road
Childs Hill
London NW2 2AT
Tel: 020 8201 9234
eurojpn@aol.com
www.eurojapanlinks.co.uk
Japanese textiles, patchwork and sashiko supplies (mail order)

Inca Studio
10 Duke Street
Princes Risborough
Bucks HP27 0AT
Tel: 01844 343 343
mail@incastudio.com
www.incastudio.com
Taupe cottons and quilting supplies (mail order and shop)

Susan Briscoe Designs
Yamadera
4 Mount Zion
Brymbo
Wrexham LL11 5NB
susan@susanbriscoe.co.uk
www.susanbriscoe.co.uk
Vintage Japanese fabrics (mail order)

Bibliography

Arts of Japan 1 – Design Motifs, Saburo Mizoguichi (Shibundō, Tokyo/Weatherhill, New York, 1973)
Beyond the Tanabata Bridge – Traditional Japanese Textiles, ed. William Jay Rathburn (Thames and Hudson/Seattle Art Museum, London, 1993)
An Illustrated Encyclopedia of Japanese Family Crests (Graphic-sha/Japan Publications, Tokyo, 2001)
Japanese Costume and Textile Arts, Seiroku Noma (Heibonsha, Tokyo/Weatherhill, New York, 1974)
Japanese Country Textiles, Anna Jackson (V&A Publications, London, 1997)
Kimono – Fashioning Culture, Lisa Dalby (Vintage, London, 2001)
Kogin and Sashiko Stitch, Kiyoko Ogikubo (Kyoto Shoin Co. Ltd, Kyoto, 1993)
Nippon no Monyo, Kazuo Kobayashi (Nippon Vogue Co., Tokyo, 1997)
Sashiko Hyakuyo, Eiko Yoshida (Bunka Shuppan Kyoku, Tokyo, 1981)
Snow, Wave, Pine – Traditional Patterns in Japanese Design, Sadao Hibi & Motoji Niwa (Kodansha International, Tokyo, 2001)
Traditional Japanese Small Motif, Kamon Yoshimoto (Page One Publishing, Singapore, 1993)
Tsutsugaki Textiles of Japan, Gensho Sasakura (Shikōsha, Kyoto, 1987)

Author's acknowledgements

I would like to thank everyone who kindly allowed me to feature their work in this book: Diane Abram, Julie-Elizabeth Haslam and members of Peaceful Heart Quilt Group – Chie Ikeda, Aiko Sakuraba and Yukari Domon, and Reiko Domon for sending their work. Special thanks to the staff at Ichiroya and Izuho Horiuchi for kasuri pattern advice; Nina Conrad at Clover Europe for supplying colourful bias tapes for appliqué; Michael Oakshott for his beautiful Colourshott fabric used for the meisen blocks; Carlos Lucero at Robert Kaufman Fabrics for tracking down the border fabric for the quilt top on page 12; and Bernina – my 153 Quilter's Edition sewing machine stitched everything beautifully. Finally, many thanks to all the team at Quarto, our excellent step-by-step photographer Karl Adamson, and Guy for helping with everything.

Dedication

For my quilting mentors, Val and Reiko.

Credits